Grace Poured Out

God's grace is sufficient no matter what trials we go through. He gives us all the strength we need to overcome and never give up

God bless you!
Valerie M. Herndon
2 Cor. 4: 15-18

Grace Poured Out

Valerie M. Herndon

ISBN-13: 978-0-9906322-0-7
ISBN-10: 0-9906322-0-2

First Flight Publishing

Printed in the United States of America

A portion of the book proceeds go to:
International Medical Outreach. A ministry that concentrates it's
efforts towards the relief of infectious diseases including intestinal
parasites, malaria, HIV/AIDS and other diseases. Their website is:
www.imoutreach.com

A Transforming Touch

"It was late in the evening when we received a call about Katie being taken to the hospital. The cancer had returned with a vengeance. I knew the Herndon's from church, but did not really know Katie. When Valerie asked Laurie if we would come pray for her, we did it without hesitation.

I remember preparing to walk into her room after washing my hands with disinfectant. We stood there with her family and Katie—she was sedated, and there was a spirit of heaviness and fear that was palpable.

Then came the moment when I stepped forward, laid my hands on her and it happened! I know you are hoping there was some supernatural power coming through my hands and she sprung out of bed and ran around the room. But no, as I laid hands on Katie—something happened to me! There was such an overwhelming feeling of peace. I felt a connectedness to this young girl. There was a presence of God in her that was so palpable, that as I laid hands on her, she poured out God's grace on me.

There are some experiences in life when someone comes to minister or care for you in a time of need. There are other times when we have the opportunity to reach out to someone in the midst of tragedy and provide comfort. Then there are those rare times when we reach out to someone in the midst of their darkest hour and find ourselves being impacted and comforted in ways that are difficult to explain. This was one of those rare times.

For the next thirty days, I visited or spoke with Katie every day. I experienced the lows and the pain that came with the treatments and I experienced the highs that came through glimpses of progress and the amazing dreams that the Lord gave her through the journey.

It was clear that through this tragically painful experience Katie had developed an intimacy with Jesus that many would think is unachievable this side of heaven. This is a book about that journey. It will make you laugh, it will most certainly make you cry—but more importantly it will give you hope. Hope that regardless of how dark your circumstances the Lord is real, He is alive and He will be there to comfort and sustain you.

Grace Poured Out is about the life of an amazing young lady in her journey through the dark valley we call cancer. It is about the grace of God that was poured out on a family during their time of unspeakable grief. But more significantly, it is also about the tangible grace of God that was poured out through Katie to everyone who experienced the miracle of knowing her."

Forever changed,
Duncan Dodds

I am so glad that I met beautiful Katie and was able to be with her for a short time. I saw a loving family fighting a battle and their strength was amazing. They trusted Jesus the whole way and were remarkable. I got a call one night about 9:00 from our good friend Duncan Dodds telling me that they were at the hospital and Katie was not doing well. I went immediately and when I saw all the people in ICU, I knew this young lady was well loved. Her room was filled with friends and relatives. So precious! After I prayed and started to leave, I wanted to kiss Katie on the forehead but I couldn't reach her. Duncan picked me up and held me over the bed rail and I kissed her. I left the hospital thinking, "What a family!"

Katie evidently had a glimpse of heaven and she chose to go. What a life she lived in that short time. I know for sure that Jesus is a good babysitter and He will take good care of His special little girl.

I salute the Herndon family. They are great people.

Dodie Osteen,
Co-Founder of Lakewood Church

Grace Poured Out *overflows with raw honesty and courage. It's a family's journey of faith, hope and love; a spiritual awakening to accept God's grace and to trust Him…no matter what. This is more than a book about grief, it's a story of restoration and an account of God's insurmountable grace. We stand in awe of their strength and how He used the pain and struggles of losing Katie to strengthen their family and resurrect a lifeless marriage.* Grace Poured Out *draws you in; we read it cover to cover and couldn't put it down. It is a must-read for families and married couples everywhere.*

Richard and Sheri Bright,
owners of marriagefunatics.com

Valerie is a woman with heart and passion. She loves deeply and writes honestly. She writes from a place that can only come from someone who has experienced the compassion, love and grace of our Heavenly Father. This book will touch everyone because we all need to know the reality of God's unlimited and matchless grace upon grace.

Laurie Dodds, author of *Regret, Rehearse, Rejoice and Identity Theft, Who's Life are You Living Anyway?*

If the storms of life have you feeling devastated and faltering in your faith, this book is for you! In this intimate journey through the loss of their daughter to cancer, we are reminded that God is present in our darkest valleys and His plans are always good, even when we don't understand. Let this book minister to your soul and strengthen your hope in God!

Steve Austin, Senior Director, Lakewood Church

This book is a selfless act of love that will encourage, strengthen and inspire us all to persevere in our darkest hours of life. I think we should all read it to bolster us even before life's storms come crashing against us.

Titus Venyah, MD

Grace Poured Out *is a moving account of a fifteen-year-old girl's courageous battle with bone cancer and the family that rallied beside her.*

Twelve years after Katie's death, Valerie Herndon has graciously shared a mother's perspective of that journey with us. And what emerges from the grief and heartache arising out of the loss of her daughter is a beautiful story of love, hope and grace. By sharing their story, Valerie gives us an invaluable guide for navigating the inevitable seasons of loss. This book will be a tremendous asset for those on a similar path or anyone who has endured the heartache of losing a loved one. Thank you, Valerie.

Paul Osteen, MD

Grace Poured Out *will touch your heart, feed your soul and bless you in ways beyond imagination. In this inspiring book, Valerie Herndon shares the pain of losing their daughter to cancer, but also the joy of having un-wavering faith, despite the circumstances. No matter what battle you may be facing* Grace Poured Out *will give you insight, inspiration, and hope to keep moving forward.*

Michelle Prince
Ziglar Certified Speaker
Best-Selling Author

DEDICATION

This book is dedicated to all who have experienced deep loss. May you find hope here and in a saving knowledge of Jesus Christ.

Acknowledgments

Thank you to Janet Long who worked wonders putting this book together. You really exceeded my expectations.

My sincere thanks to Michelle Prince who unselfishly focuses on the success of others. May all your wildest dreams come true!

Thank you Cindy Kruse-Ratcliff and the Lakewood church choir for carrying us with your music all these years. What a gift you are to the body of Christ.

Steve Austin, thank you for giving me that last shove over the writing mountain. You are such an encourager and I appreciate your forthrightness.

Dr Paul Osteen, you have impacted us way more than you realize. Thanks for pushing us out of the boat and into the deep.

Thank you Dodie Osteen for having the biggest heart for people I've ever seen. You are a shining example to us all.

Thank you to Duncan and Laurie Dodds. Your wise and godly counsel was and still is invaluable to us. I'm so thankful God intersected our paths. You are awesome people.

To all my friends and workout buddies. I love hanging out and having fun win you. You are my therapy!

To my dearest friends Debbie and Doug Schultz. I fell in love the first time I met you and haven't stopped since! I appreciate all that you've done for us and I know you miss Katie almost as much as we do.

Thank you to Richard and Sheri Bright who keep us laughing.

Every week in class is a joy ride. You are our biggest cheerleaders and we appreciate all your support.

To our awesome Sunday school class. We feel it a huge privilege to share life with you and still scratch our heads because you actually want to hear more. Thank you for cheering us on.

To all my family near and far. Thank you for the many hours you prayed for us. I love you all dearly and I know that our loss was your loss.

Nick and Bethany, you truly are gifts from God. I want to thank you for your contributions to the book. You did very well but even better in choosing your marriage partners. We thank God every day for them. Love you bunches.

To my precious husband, Wes. Man, did I ever hit the jackpot! Thank you for all your support, patience and help in getting me through this project. Thank you for letting me bounce things off of you. I love growing old with you and love you with all my heart. You're the best friend I've ever had.

My deepest thanks goes to my Lord and Savior Jesus Christ. You're the reason I'm still here. If it weren't for you I wouldn't have made it. I'm looking forward to the day when I see your beautiful face.

FOREWORD

We each have those "why" and "why not" moments in our lives. This is the story of one of those moments. Why does cancer strike a young person? Why do families that are serving the Lord have struggles and challenges? Why does God allow the death of a vibrant young girl, when it appears that her full healing and recovery would bring such glory to Him? Why Katie and not me?

CHAPTER 1

LIFE INTERRUPTED

"Mom, my knee hurts," Katie said after practice one day. She was on the junior high track team and had just finished basketball season the week before.

"You just need to rest and ice it for a while," I said, thinking it was an overuse injury.

"I want to quit track," she said, "I'm tired of it."

I said, "No, you need to finish the last few weeks." Wes and I were sticklers about our kids finishing what they started.

I should have paid more attention. I should have listened. After working as a P.E. teacher all day, all I wanted to do was get supper ready, finish the laundry, and crash. I didn't want to stop doing what I needed to get done long enough to really listen. We were a typical family, living life at breakneck speed.

My husband, Wes, was on the church council, served as president of the school board, and worked long hours. We were living two separate lives, and our marriage was mediocre at best. Wes and I rarely took time for ourselves or each other. We hardly communicated, unless it was something concerning the kids. For the most part, he wasn't much for conversation and only wanted the executive summary.

Sometimes, I would look at him and wonder—after 23 years of marriage—who he really was inside. He rarely showed his thoughts or feelings. This was great for him, since all he wanted was peace and quiet in the house, but it sure made for a passionless relationship. I would try to start fights with him, because, in my mind, we were at least interacting when we were fighting. We were so busy serving others, but we forgot to serve each other. We prioritized whatever our three kids were involved in at the time over everything, including our marriage.

Katie was 14, Bethany was 15, and our son, Nick, was 22, about to graduate from college. It was the spring of 2001. Katie wasn't the athlete like her sister or the intellect like her brother. She was the artistic one who loved to draw. She only played sports to be with her friends.

Katie was an affectionate child and gave hugs freely. She gave the best hugs and instinctively knew if someone needed one. Even as a baby, she would just sort out of melt into the chest of whoever was holding her.

Katie would say the funniest things, too. When she was four years old, I took her with me to the salon when I needed to get a lip wax. She watched intently as the lady smeared the hot brown wax on one side of my lip. Her mouth dropped, and her eyes got as big as golf balls.

She slapped her hands to her cheeks and shouted, "Oh no! She's a man!"

Everyone in the salon was cracking up. She never tried to be funny; she just was.

Another time, I was losing patience being cooped up with two active preschoolers. I was craving some alone time and told Katie to go color with her sister. She shook her head no. I asked her why she didn't want to play with her sister.

Her reply was, "I don't want to get in trouble."

She had a point, since that's usually how most of their playtimes ended up.

She was kind of a shy child, although she didn't shy away from the stage. She didn't need to be the center of attention, but her dream in junior high was to move to Hollywood and become a movie star. She loved hamming it up in school plays, especially in comedic roles. Katie was always thinking of others, too. She was genuinely happy if others won awards or good things came their way. When she was five and Bethany six, we had given Bethany a new bicycle for her birthday.

Katie was so excited for Bethany and told her, "Now, it's even! You have a bike, and I have roller skates!"

She was kind-hearted and generous. She was always giving her stuff away.

But, she had her faults, too. Her worst one was stubbornness. If she didn't want to do something, she wasn't going to do it. No amount of discipline, coercing, bribing, or begging could change her mind. Most of the time, she was a compliant child, but if her mind was made up about something, there was no use fighting with her about it. This stubbornness frustrated us, but God would later turn that stubbornness into determination. She was going to need every bit of it in the battle she would soon be facing.

Katie rarely complained. Of my three children, she was the least demanding. Soon, though, she would be the one demanding every bit of our attention. Katie was limping constantly, and her knee started getting red, swollen and hot to the touch. I took her in for an appointment.

"Mrs. Herndon, looking at her knee, this looks like it could be a bone fracture or maybe an infection. I won't know for sure until Katie has a bone scan done. In the meantime, she needs to stay off that knee and ice it a few times a day to keep the swelling down," the doctor said.

The imaging place was packed. My mind was racing with the list piling up in my head.

Bethany has private lessons at 3:00. I have to pick her up at 5:00, and then I need to drop the girls off at youth group at 6:45.

Oh, man, I forgot to call the exterminator again.

Swing by and pick up the dry cleaning on the way home.

What else do I need from the store for supper tonight?

Why is this taking so long?

I really need to get going.

I was so unaware, so preoccupied that the thought of this being serious never crossed my mind. I was about to experience the biggest interruption of a lifetime.

I don't know how I'm going to play at camp. My knee hurts so bad I can't even walk on it! The pain never goes away. It's always there. Pounding and throbbing—it feels like someone pounding on it with a hammer, shattering it. I don't know how much longer I can stand it. It hurts so bad.

KATIE'S JOURNAL ENTRY, MAY 26, 2001

CHAPTER 2

THE PHONE CALL

A few days later, I was helping clean up the home of a family who had severe flooding after tropical storm Allison. Wes agreed to take Katie in for her follow-up to get the bone scan results. Before the doctor said anything, he wanted x-rays done.

Afterwards, he came in and said, "Dad, can I speak with you outside for a moment?" They went into his office and shut the door behind them. "Your daughter has a tumor over her entire knee. I'm referring her to a cancer doctor at Texas Children's Hospital. She needs to get a biopsy done right away."

My cell phone rang.

"Hey, Hon, what'd the doctor say?" I asked.

"She has a tumor on her knee," Wes said.

I thought he was joking. "Wes, stop playing around." It was the furthest thing from my mind.

This time, he was much more forceful in his answer. "Valerie, I'm not playing around. The doctor said she has a tumor on her knee."

I had a hard time believing what he was telling me. *Cancer? What? No! Cancer doesn't run on either side of the family. No, that can't be it. Anyway, this only happens to old people who smoke—not 14-year-old girls.*

When I got home, I hugged Katie for a long time. I told her, "Honey, don't worry. God is going to take care of you. This is just a minor inconvenience, and we'll get through it." She hugged me back, didn't say a word, and limped off.

I was so naive. It turned out to be a lot more than just an inconvenience.

OVERWHELMED

I began asking for prayer requests from a few faithful friends who I knew would pray. I was amazed at how it spread like wildfire. People were praying as far away as Australia. It touched our family in a profound way. The only problem was all this took place before Facebook, Twitter, and other social media. When the news got out, people were calling us constantly.

"Yes, thank you for asking, we appreciate your concern. Yes, she's taking a nap right now (wish I could). I'll try and keep you posted," I said for the thousandth time. "Wes, I'm so tired of all these calls."

"Well, take the phone off the hook, and go get some rest," he said.

"I can't," I replied. "I'm waiting for the doctor's office to call to set up her biopsy." I wished they would hurry up. I could feel the knots in my shoulders. People were so kind with their concern, but I got tired of repeating myself over and over. Looking back, I needed someone who could have fielded all those calls. I knew they meant well, but it was exhausting. I'm sure I offended some people, but, unless you've been through anything like that, it's hard to understand. Nowadays, there's a wonderful website called *Care Pages* to help with medical updates and taking care of the needs of patients, which would have been helpful.

I saw a boy on his bike today. I watched him with envy. I miss doing the simplest things in life: running, walking, jumping, being free from pain. The doctor told me today when I was at my check-up how my knee was. He said he wasn't sure what it was. He said it may be a tumor.

I never figured these kinds of things would happen to me. Sure I broke my arm a couple of times, got stung by a jelly fish, but nothing like this. I'm not sure what I'm going to tell my friends.

KATIE'S JOURNAL ENTRY, JUNE 15,

NIGHTS WERE THE WORST

The doctor prescribed Vicodin, because her pain had gotten so bad. It barely took the edge off. Later that evening, Wes and I prayed over her and put her to bed. I woke up at 4:30 the next morning to check on her and found her crying.

"Mom, my knee hurts so bad."

"Katie, how long have you been up?" I asked.

She started crying harder. "All night."

I got in bed with her and prayed for her again. I thought to myself, *Why isn't that stupid Vicodin working?! Please, God, can't you take the pain away? I hate seeing my child suffer!*

She finally settled down and fell asleep. ♣

CHAPTER 3

THE BIOPSY

T he next day, Katie was scheduled for her biopsy. Our friends Jim and Elayne Slater went with us, and we were glad to have them there. Jim prayed for Katie's healing, and Elayne, a registered nurse, translated this new medical language that was so foreign to us. Katie went in around 8:00 that morning. I'm not sure how long it took, but we were there for hours.

When the doctor came out, he said he was about 80% sure it was malignant. He said it would have to be sent off to confirm his suspicions. In the meantime, he was referring us to another cancer doctor who would oversee Katie's treatments. I was hoping he was wrong and thought to myself, *We still have a 20% chance it's not cancer.*

He said she needed to get started on chemotherapy right away. The doctor said the clinic would call me the next day to set up our first consultation.

When we got home from her biopsy, Katie went straight to bed. During the night, the block that kept her from having pain wore off, and she was up all night again crying in pain. I got up around 6:00 a.m. to check on her.

"Katie, have you been on your back this whole time?"

"Yes," she whimpered.

"You need to roll over on your side for a while."

"No, Mom," she said. "I can't."

"Honey, you've got to," I pleaded.

"No, it hurts too much," she said between sobs.

Gently, I slid both arms under her knee and held it until she stopped crying. She hesitated and then slowly rolled over. She had been on her back for 18 hours. I got in bed with her. I prayed for her healing and strength for us both. I just didn't know how I was going to cope with all of this. I was unprepared for how much bigger my troubles were about to get.

> On Thursday I went in for the biopsy. It was kinda scary. They put me to sleep with a gas mask, but I could still feel the needle (from the IV) going into my arm right before I fell asleep. When I woke up, they had put the central line into my chest. It's like a large wire that sticks out of my chest, and forks into two tubes. It's really freaky looking. I was pretty much helpless on Friday. My dad fed me chicken rice soup and apple juice. The pain in my chest and knee left me almost useless. I couldn't leave my bed the whole day.

> That night I was up till the crack of dawn crying. The pain was terrible. Mom came in and comforted me. Grandma sent me a comic drawing book with jelly beans and chocolate drizzled popcorn. (I gave mom the popcorn—it's her favorite). Friday night I slept on the couch. I didn't do anything Saturday—I was still in pain. Monday I didn't do much. Tuesday I went to a swim party. I sat around and watched everyone swim. It wasn't much fun. I go in to see the cancer dude tomorrow to see when I start my treatment and how long it will be.

KATIE'S JOURNAL ENTRY, JUNE 25, 2002

THE CONSULTATION

"Katie, are you up yet?" My volume was getting louder after repeating myself. "Hurry up, or we'll be late!"

She labored getting around on crutches and would tire so easily. It seemed like it took us forever to get anywhere, and I was losing my patience with her. It was an hour drive to Texas Children's Hospital. We walked into the cancer clinic for the first time. I couldn't believe my eyes. There in our midst was a sea of bald-headed kids running around everywhere. It was odd to me that they were all so happy. I felt sadness come over me when I remembered reading the statistic that one in ten children would die from cancer that year. I felt sorry for the moms in that room. It never dawned on me that Katie could be one of those statistics.

"Katie Herndon!" The nurse yelled above the roar. We inched our way to the back room. A man and woman joined us.

"Hello, Katie. I'm Dr. Marali, and this is Melody, the nurse practitioner. We'll be helping you with your treatments. It's nice to meet you, Katie." Katie gave them a half smile.

Dr. Marali looked at Wes and me and said, "The biopsy confirms your daughter has Osteosarcoma. The tumor is covering the entire knee and inside it, too. It's very uncommon for young girls to get this type of bone cancer. It usually happens in young boys, mostly African-American."

I thought to myself, *No, Lord, why couldn't this just be a bone infection or stress fracture like the doctors first told us? NOT THIS! NOT CANCER!*

I couldn't believe what he was telling us. This was my worst nightmare. I wished I had made her appointment sooner and not put it off. I was mad at myself for letting so many insignificant things get in the way.

I got up the courage to ask the question, but I was almost afraid to hear the answer. "What are her chances?"

Dr. Marali said, "Very good. The survival rate is good with this type of cancer."

I felt relieved, but then he continued.

"Nevertheless, she could have some very bad side effects from the chemo that we use."

"Like what?" I asked. He handed me a sheet. The list was long. I read it out loud. "Hair loss, mouth sores, fatigue, depression, dry mouth, nausea, vomiting, neutropenia (low white blood cells), anemia (low red blood cells), low platelets, infection and fever from neutropenia, red splotchy skin, body aches, bruising, mood swings from the steroids, uncontrollable shaking, no appetite, tasting metal or no taste at all, possible loss of hearing, and weight loss."

When I finished, Melody said, "The chemo could affect her heart, too. The way we treat cancer is very barbaric, but it's the best treatment we have right now."

This does sound barbaric, I thought to myself.

Dr. Marali said, "Katie will also have a total knee replacement surgery called limb salvage nine to ten weeks into chemo. The standard used to be total amputation of the leg. Also, it's probably best if you go ahead and cut off her hair so it won't be so traumatic when it starts falling out."

I looked at Katie's silky, long, black hair. I choked back the tears. I knew I didn't have the luxury of falling apart now. It would have to wait.

Katie looked down at the ground, not saying a word.

"Before she starts chemo," Dr. Marali continued, "she needs to have her central lines put in. These are two plastic tubes inserted into her chest where she'll receive all her meds and have her blood drawn. It will keep her from getting stuck with needles so much."

The thought of that grossed me out. Tubes coming out of her chest?

"The first thing she will need to do is have all her baseline testing done," Dr. Marali said. "She needs an audiogram, echocardiogram, MRI, GFR for kidney functions, and a bone density test. *Then*, we start chemo. But, for today, I want you to go to her orthodontist and have those braces taken off."

I protested, "Why? She's only had them on for a month."

Then, Melody explained that the chemo she would be taking could cause mouth sores that could be aggravated by the metal in her mouth.

This is too much, God! I'm not that strong! I was so overwhelmed. There was so much information to absorb.

"Here's my cell phone number if you need me for anything or have any questions," Melody said. I appreciated that.

We left downtown and went straight to the orthodontist around 7:00 that evening. We watched as Katie had her braces removed. She was quiet when we got in the car. I could tell she was holding stuff in.

Not me; I cried the whole ride home. It was then that I realized I couldn't do this alone. I needed God so desperately. Little did I know, that day in the doctor's office, how the typical busy life that I knew would be turned upside down. I would need every ounce of God's grace poured out on me. ♣

CHAPTER 4

GOD WORKING BEHIND THE SCENES

K atie's sister, Bethany, was 15 at the time and played competitive volleyball year-round. In the summer, she attended volleyball camp. While we were there, I met Sue Schelfhout who coached in a private school and was helping with the camp. Sue was an all-American setter for the University of Texas. Bethany had a dream of becoming a setter for a Division 1 college. Sue and I struck up a conversation when she found out about Katie.

"Hey, Valerie, I heard Bethany was transferring to public school this fall. She really needs to be in a place where she would have a community of people who would take care of her. She's going to need that when Katie starts having treatments."

"Oh, Sue," I said. "We would give anything for Bethany to play for you."

"Anything is possible," she said.

I laughed and said, "Not on our budget!"

Sue said, "Why don't you fill out the financial aid paperwork and see if you qualify?" She called me after camp was over to let us know they still had some financial aid available for us. We were ecstatic. Sue would prove to be not only a great coach to Bethany, but a great mentor as well. The parents there were invaluable to us the following year during our hardest time. They literally took Bethany under their wing and treated her as their own. They were another example of God's grace being poured out on us.

BIG BROTHER

Nick had passed the LSAT and planned on entering the University of Houston law school that fall. He and Katie were very close, and, after he got the news, he decided to put off law school, get a job, and live at home to spend more time with her. I was apprehensive at first, afraid he would decide to never go back, but it turned out to be a wise decision. There were so many times I needed to run errands, and he and Katie would just hang out and watch their favorite Japanese anime, *Cowboy Bebop*. ♣

CHAPTER 5

LIFE ON ANOTHER PLANET

After a week of getting all her tests done, the day of Katie's first surgery arrived. This was to insert the central lines into her chest. After a few days of recovering at home, the Home Health Care nurses came out to the house to show me how to change the dressing on her central lines. No matter how tired or busy I was, her lines had to be flushed out every day with a special solution to keep them from getting clogged or infected. If they ever got clogged, it would mean another surgery to replace them. I was getting my first exposure to becoming a full-time nurse. I hated everything about nursing. I couldn't stand needles, blood, or vomit, and I was about to experience more than my fair share of all three of them.

Katie's first chemo treatment would start July third. We would be spending the week of July Fourth in the hospital, while everyone we knew would be shooting off fireworks. While leaving to go to the hospital, we went through the laundry room and noticed the floor was flooded.

"Wes, why is there water all over the floor?" I asked.

"I think the washing machine is leaking," he said.

I was so irritated. It wasn't even that old of a machine. I didn't know how many days we would be staying in the hospital, and I would have to deal with this when we got home. Elayne offered to wash a couple of loads for me while we were in the hospital. I was too embarrassed to have her wash my underwear, so I did it myself by hand in the bathroom sink during our stay.

We arrived at the clinic early that morning to check into the hospital only to wait eight hours for them to have a room open up for Katie. During this waiting period, Katie began to draw more and more. It became her therapy. It kept her mind off the intensity and gruesomeness of what she was about to face.

Finally, they called us up and sent us to the ninth floor of the hospital. Wow…the ninth floor…this is where our reality hit us between the eyes: the smell, beeping cancer machines, and some very sick kids. This was all so foreign to us that it felt like we were on another planet altogether.

Late that afternoon, the nurses started her IV. It took four hours to hydrate Katie before they actually started the chemo at 10:00 p.m. I was surprised they started it so late at night, but cancer doesn't stop and neither did those wonderful nurses.

After hydrating Katie, she had three more doses of chemo and another four hours of hydration at the end. Right away, Katie turned a pale yellowish color. It really got to me at first. She started throwing up the next day. I eventually got used to it and could read her body language so well she didn't even have to ask for the pink dishpan anymore.

Staying in the hospital was a challenge. We got very little sleep, because it never got quiet. There were so many interruptions during the night, too. I couldn't believe the number of people checking on her. This was around-the-clock care. On any given day in the hospital, she would be visited by the oncologist, the PA (physician's assistant), the sociologist, the adolescent doctor, several nurses, the charge nurse, the child life specialist, fellows and med students in residency, some lady about her school work, a nutritionist, and volunteers handing out gifts. To top it off, Texas Children's is a teaching hospital, so we had a steady flow of medical students wanting to interview us and Katie's history.

We never had a full hour to ourselves. We always felt ecstatic when we could go home and sleep in our own beds again. ꙮ

CHAPTER 6

DEBBIE SCHULTZ

M y good friend Debbie Schultz and her daughter, Lauren, came by on our first day in the hospital with gifts and food items. We were so glad to see them. Debbie called the next day to check on Katie. I was thankful for faithful friends. She would prove to be among the best.

Katie even preferred to hang out with her more than anyone

else. Since her daughter was good friends with Katie, she spent a lot of time at their house and they were like family to her. Sometimes, she would ask if Mrs. Schultz could come over and play video games with her while I went out and ran some errands. Many times, I would tell her I didn't have any errands to run. She would make up things for me to do. I think she was trying to ditch mom for Mrs. Schultz.

Katie loved having her go to clinic visits with us, because, afterwards, she would treat us to any restaurant Katie wanted. Debbie would order way more food than any of us could eat, and we always got to take home leftovers. Debbie was—and still is—one of the most giving people I have ever known.

One visit, she brought so much food that we filled up all the drawers in the cabinet in Katie's room and the community refrigerator. We were sharing with anyone who would take it. It was a ridiculous amount of food.

She has taught me a lot about generosity—not with just money, but also with time. Katie and I would be careful saying anything around her, because she would immediately run out and get it. She went with me so many times to the clinic and hospital, I lost count.

HELP NEEDED

There were many other people, mainly from our church and the place where Wes worked, who donated time and meals. One friend came over and worked on my flower beds, weeding, watering, and trimming. I had quite a few roses, and she took care of them for me. This same friend gave me $500.00 towards valet parking. I put it aside for just that, but, with so many visits to Texas Children's, we went through it pretty quickly.

A couple of other friends arranged for me to have a massage. Another friend coordinated meals for the 16 months Katie was in treatment. It was such a blessing to come home to a home cooked meal after a long, draining day of clinic or hospital visits. The parents at Bethany's school also stepped in and made sure she was taken care of. We never had to worry about her. I can't imagine going through this alone. All these wonderful people were more evidence of God's grace being poured out on us. &

CHAPTER 7

OUR NEW NORMAL

I started to find chunks of Katie's hair all over the house. There were piles of it everywhere, even after cutting it off. Before she went completely bald, we went to get her fitted for a wig. There wasn't much to choose from in styles that looked good on 14-year-old girls. These were old lady wigs. She found one that she didn't hate too much.

I asked her, "Do you like this one, Katie?"

She said flatly, "I look like an anchorwoman."

I looked at her reflection in the mirror. Katie was right. She looked like she could do the evening news. She hardly wore the thing and opted instead for the bald bandana look.

WES GIVING HER SHOTS

Katie was given a Lupron shot in the hospital to stop her menstrual cycle. This had to be done since her platelets would be knocked down from the chemo. Platelets are the sticky stuff that causes your blood to clot. The GCFS shot was to be given after a round of che-mo to build up her white blood counts after those were also knocked down. This had to be done every day until her counts were back up. To save another hour-long trip to the clinic, Wes offered to give her the GCFS shots. He would come home at lunch and give her the shot in her thigh. I didn't have the stomach for it.

It's weird how one thing can change your life so dramatically. I'm so close to my parents now. I like it better.

The chemo treatments are hard. They make me sick and lose my hair. I have to homeschool this year because of treatments, but this way it is easier. I guess cancer really has been a life-changing experience. I have to de-pend on so many people. I no longer seclude myself from the world. I cherish my family even more, and every day is a blessing.

It's so heartbreaking watching all the babies and toddlers coming in for treatment. I wish I was more like them. They laugh and smile and run around like nothing's wrong.

After this, I believe I'll be a much stronger person. I no longer care what my peers think. I don't pay much attention to my looks or weight. I just hang out with them as I am.

The cancer gives you a new outlook on life. But, it's still very tough to go through.

KATIE'S JOURNAL ENTRY, SEPTEMBER 6, 2001

9/11: A VERY SAD DAY

Katie was scheduled for another round of chemo on 9/11. We were heading out the door to go to the clinic when Wes called.

"Hey, have you been watching the news?" he asked.

"No, why?" I was surprised by his question.

"Someone flew an airplane into the World Trade Center this morning. They think it's terrorists. They've shut down the Medical Center. I don't think you should go in this morning."

The local news reports were telling people to stay home unless they had a medical emergency. I was afraid to go, but Katie qualified as a medical emergency. We had no choice. It was creepy when we were the only car driving towards downtown. It looked like all of Houston was racing to get home.

When we got to the clinic, there were only a handful of patients there. I will never forget this moment as long as I live. As the nurse was drawing blood from Katie, we were all glued to the TV. The South Tower had already fallen, and we sat in horror when the North Tower crumbled to the ground. We were so relieved when we found out that Katie's blood counts weren't high enough for chemo that day. All we wanted to do was get home and stay home.

KATIE NEEDS DRANO

Every day, I would flush her central lines. There were many times I would forget until nighttime, and then I would fight laziness and have to force myself to do it.

One day, I just could not get the lines cleared out. Katie couldn't go a day without it being flushed because of the risk for infection. So, that meant an unexpected hour-long drive to the clinic. When we got there, the nurse put some stuff in her lines they referred to as Drano. It had to be left in there for two hours, and then she would try flushing it.

It was stuck. She told us to try again tomorrow, so we drove back the next day. It wouldn't budge. Since her total knee replacement was scheduled in a few days, they decided to put in a new central line at the same time as her knee surgery. ♣

CHAPTER 8

THE BIG SURGERY

The day came for Katie's knee replacement surgery. She was nervous but was so tired of living with all the pain, that she was ready for it. However, we didn't realize how much more pain she would be having and how hard her recovery was going to be.

Six inches of her femur bone were removed with a total knee replacement. It was a five-hour surgery, plus another hour to replace her central lines. We left the house at 5:30 that morning. We consulted with six doctors before she was wheeled back into the operating room. She would now have to be in a wheelchair full-time.

I have a whole new perspective on people in wheelchairs. It would frustrate me when people would park in handicapped spaces and didn't have a handicap hang tag.

The surgeon came out when he was done and said, "It looks like I got all the cancer. Her femur bone was so strong, I had to split it to get the prosthesis in. Because of that, her recovery will be a little longer until the bones set and the soft tissue heals. You can go back and see her now."

When we walked into the recovery room, my heart sank. She was so pale. Katie was still sleeping and heavily sedated. She looked like the Bionic Woman with all the tubes, machines, and wires hooked up to her. I was checking everything out trying to formulate a plan for her recovery in my head. How was she going to use the potty? Or sleep at night? Would she be strong enough in three to four weeks for the butt-kicking chemo?

I saw the surgeon had inserted her new central line right next to her breast. He wasn't able to use the original entry, because it had so much bacteria colonizing around it.

"Great," I sighed. "One more thing we have to deal with."

RECOVERY FLOOR

They sent Katie to the eleventh floor to recover. It was a lot quieter than the cancer floor, and we were thankful. She had a pain pump with her, but it didn't seem to help.

"Mom, this hurts so bad," she cried.

I felt helpless. "Katie, if I could, I would take this all off of you and put it on me," I said.

She wiped her tears and said, "I know you would, Mom."

During a quiet moment, I asked God, *Why Katie? I don't understand. Why does she have to go through all this?*

Then I heard Him say, *Why not Katie?*

I thought about that a long time. I didn't have an answer. The only thing I could do now was pray and lean into Him more. I had to come to a place of total dependence on God's grace to get me through.

A few days later, her foot became very sensitive because of all the nerve damage. She couldn't stand anyone touching it or even going near it.

"Mom, don't! It hurts too much!" she said.

"Katie, the physical therapist said for me to exercise your foot to relieve some of the swelling," I said, wishing I didn't have to hurt her so much. Tears rolled down her cheeks. I felt a lump in my throat and knots in my shoulders.

Lord, help me! I can't stand doing this! I screamed on the inside. Going to the restroom was a challenge, even with a potty chair, because of the searing pain and her being unable to bend her knee. We were in the hospital for eight days. The doctor wouldn't release her until she could take a few steps with her walker.

The day before we were dismissed, a cool front had blown in, and Katie wanted to go outside. She was so thankful to get out of the hospital for a while, and we lingered in the crisp air. It's amazing how much the little things mean when they've been taken away for a while.

Even to this day, when I pass a hospital, I say, "Thank you, Lord, that I'm not in the hospital," and whisper a prayer for all the people there. ❧

CHAPTER 9

NURSE AND BOLD FRIEND, ELAYNE

While we were staying on the eleventh floor, a family checked into the room next to us. I could hear the toddler crying off and on. Our friends, Jim and Elayne, were visiting Katie that night. When the nurse came in to check Katie's vitals, I asked her if that baby next door was okay.

She said, "Yes, he's by himself, and he's just scared."

"How old is he?" I asked.

"18 months," she said.

I asked, "Why is he by himself?"

She said, "Because the parents left and told us to take care of him. We've all been taking turns holding him."

We were all floored. Elayne got really upset. She bolted out the door and went looking for the parents. She found the dad outside the hospital slouched against the wall smoking a cigarette.

She told him, "Sir, you can't leave your baby up there by himself!" The distraught man looked up at her and said, "Ma'am, I can't handle this. It's too much for me!"

"You better handle it," she said. "That baby should not be left alone like that! He's your responsibility, not the nurse's!"

He took one last puff and slowly went back upstairs to take care of his son. The dad never left his room again until his son was released. We never saw the mom.

Another time, Elayne went with us to get some important scans done. She was standing on one side of Katie, and I was on the other. We were talking and laughing when the technician came in and asked, "Oh, are you sisters?"

Before I could say anything, Elayne blurted out, "Yes! She's the older one."

"What? You've got ten years on me!" I said.

We were going back and forth for a while. It helped ease the tension—at least, for the moment.

One day, we pulled into the hospital for a chemo treatment, and I really appreciated my bold friend. Katie was feeling nauseous and ready to get out of the car. Traffic was deadlocked. Elayne got tired of waiting and jumped out of the car. She started motioning for cars to move over so I could pull in closer to the curb. I was embarrassed, because a lot of people were also waiting to drop off patients, but she sure made things easier for us.

However, her take-charge attitude almost got her into trouble with the doctor on one visit. Elayne, Katie, and I were listening as the doctor was explaining what was going on with the results of Katie's latest blood tests. Since Elayne was a registered nurse, she wanted to make sure Katie and I understood his "Doctorese." She abruptly cut him off, looked at us, and translated what he had just said.

He looked over the rim of his glasses and asked sternly, "And who are you?" I almost burst out laughing, but I didn't want to get the same stink eye.

"I'm her sister," she said. Even though she irritated the doctor, I was so glad to have her there.

When we left, I told Elayne, "I can't believe you told the doctor we were sisters!"

She chuckled and said, "Well, we are—sisters in the Lord!"

I guess that wasn't a total lie. ♣

CHAPTER 10

THE IMPORTANCE OF PRAYER

One thing I learned through all of this is the importance and power of prayer. For the most part, I used to be pretty casual in my prayer life. It mostly consisted of "bless-me-Lord" kind of prayers, unless the enemy had really ticked me off about something. They were more of a defensive mode than offensive, reactive more than proactive.

Those days, I was getting a lot more aggressive in my prayer life, and I began speaking directly to the enemy to get his hands off of Katie. On one of the days that Debbie Schultz called me at the hospital to check up on Katie, God showed me just how powerful our prayers really are. Before we hung up, she offered to pray for Katie. When she began praying, I had a vision of this huge warrior completely dressed in heavy metal from head to toe. He had a three-foot-long shield he held up against the enemy and was swinging what looked like a three-foot-long, thick, heavy metal sword. It had a sharp point, and I could hear loud clanging noises as this warrior attacked the enemy. I heard this swoosh-swoosh sound as he swung his sword in a figure eight pattern. He was winning the battle and wasn't retreating. After she finished praying, I told Debbie about the vision, and we were both very encouraged when we hung up that day. It would not be the only time I had that vision. Every morning when we were at home, I had a routine. I would get up around five o'clock to go check on Katie, and, if she didn't need anything, I would get my cup of coffee, go read my Bible, and pray. One morning, I sat down on the sofa, collecting my thoughts and prioritizing my day. I remember just sitting there, and, as my thoughts started to focus on the Lord, I had the vision of the warrior again. Only this time, he was just standing there, sword and shield down by his side.

I said out loud, "Lord, who is that?"

I heard Him say, *That's a warring angel.*

"Well, why is he just standing there?" I said.

The Lord said, *He's waiting for your command!*

As soon as I started to pray, I saw the angel do the same exact thing, holding his shield up and swinging his sword around. It was a powerful vision, and, to this day, it encourages me to know that God is always fighting for me.

FAITH ON A TRUCK

One day on the way to a clinic visit, I was feeling pretty defeated. This day in particular, I had reached my limit, and I was just tired of dealing with everything. I just wanted my life back; tending to my roses, shopping, getting coffee with my friends, and especially watching Bethany's volleyball games. Deep down, I resented Wes for not being more involved with Katie's treatments. From my viewpoint, he had it easy. He would call me at the hospital all excited about how Bethany made some exciting play during her matches, and I could feel myself smoldering with anger. Why did I have to be stuck there? Wes and I had very little connection during this time, and it felt as though I was carrying this all alone while he was out having fun.

To add fuel to my fire, I was with Katie, who would be crying and pleading with God to heal her. She would tell me in between sobs she just wanted to be normal again. It tore my heart out, because I was feeling the same helpless way. For the most part, she was a trooper, so her having a meltdown affected me deeply. On this particular day, I was talking to a friend on my cell phone on the way to another endless clinic visit.

I must've sounded pretty negative, because she said to me, "Valerie, you need to have faith."

Before I could say a word, I looked at the lane on the freeway next to me, and there was a delivery truck passing me. Someone had hand painted in bold black letters, "Have faith."

I thought, *Okay, Lord, I hear you.*

That was no coincidence. I began focusing on scriptures that would build my faith more. It gave me strength to keep believing in God for a miracle. I knew I had to get control of my thoughts and allow God's grace to continue to carry me. ♣

CHAPTER 11

BUTT-KICKING CHEMO

A few weeks after Katie's knee surgery, the doctor sent us to another hospital, so they could harvest her stem cells. She would be starting the butt-kicking chemo soon. This chemo would knock her counts so low that if she got an infection or even a cold, it could be deadly. They would then do what they called a "rescue." This is where they would take her harvested stem cells they had frozen, thaw them out, and put them back into her body to "rescue" her by bringing her blood counts back up.

She was hooked up to this big machine with wires coming out of her everywhere. After being there all day long, we were so disappointed when they weren't able to get enough of her stem cells. This meant having to go through the same process all over again the next day. That time, we got enough. We were so relieved; if they hadn't harvested enough of her own stem cells, then she would have had to find a donor who matched her. I was so thankful, especially after my short conversation with a distraught woman on the elevator. Her child was on his second bone marrow transplant after his body rejected the first one. He was extremely weak, and they were having a hard time finding a match. It was not a good place to be.

THE BONE MARROW TRANSPLANT UNIT

Only three weeks after her knee replacement surgery, Katie's counts were stable enough to start the butt-kicking chemo. These were much higher doses than she'd had before. She was still recovering from surgery and was in a wheelchair full-time.

She would now be on the eighth floor, where all the sickest kids were housed. This was a much quieter floor with fewer kids, and I wondered why, until I realized their lives were constantly on the line. They weren't happy or running around playing. They just stayed in bed.

They were all neutropenic and couldn't be around a lot of people. Germs were their worst enemy. Even with very strict precautions, they could contract an infection, sometimes from within their own bodies. They didn't allow flowers on this floor because of the mold they might carry. They didn't even allow balloons. No one was allowed onto the floor without washing their hands first.

There was also a different look to the parents of these children. They were robotic in their movements and reminded me of zombies. I know it was from the intensity of what their kids were going through. It was hard to see, and I suppose I had that look, too.

While we were in the Bone Marrow Transplant Unit, Katie met her very favorite nurse, Ashley. She was never in a hurry and genuinely happy to see Katie whenever she was there. She would talk with her—not at her—and was always interested in whatever Katie was drawing at the time. I know she had other patients, but it always seemed as though Katie was her only one. Katie would light up when she saw Ashley, no matter how badly she was feeling. She was a true gift to us and happened to be a young Christian woman working with some of the sickest kids on earth. Katie would write in her journal how much she liked Ashley and always hoped she was on duty when Katie was admitted to the hospital.

The holidays were soon approaching, and we were all praying that we could have Thanksgiving at home this year and not in the hospital. I love to cook, so this was (and still is) a big holiday for us. Having my little brood around the table would have meant so much to me. God did answer our prayers. Katie didn't run any fever, but chemo was scheduled for the day after Thanksgiving.

When we were waiting to be admitted to the hospital for more chemo, we noticed an attractive woman decorating a Christmas tree. I guess she noticed us watching her, so she stopped, looked at Katie, and said, "How are you today?"

"Fine," Katie answered.

"What's your name?" the woman asked.

"Katie Herndon," she responded.

The woman introduced herself and said her name was Erin Kiltz.

"You're Erin Kiltz?" I asked.

She smiled and said, "Yes."

Erin had a daughter named Grace who was born with Down's syndrome and got cancer as a toddler. Their family spent many months in the BMT unit, and she saw firsthand the deep needs of the families around her. Many of them didn't have family or friends to help. Even though she had a great support group, she felt compassion for the other families who didn't.

Because of her experience, she started a ministry called His Grace Foundation that supplied whatever the family or cancer patients might need in the way of toiletries or personal items. Through donations, she also provided a massage therapist once a week to give neck rubs to parents and nurses who wanted them. I was usually first in line. We also received a basket of goodies the first day we arrived at the BMT unit.

My voice cracked, and I said, "Oh, we've been so blessed by your ministry. I can't tell you how much it's meant to us." We would run into Erin on occasion when she was volunteering at the hospital.

SAD NEWS

Before Katie was diagnosed, we found out that her best friend's dad was diagnosed with cancer. That meant that Brooke was tied up for the most part with her dad's treatments and didn't get to spend much time with Katie. She really missed Brooke, and Brooke really missed Katie. Katie spent several summer vacations with the family and felt very much a part of them.

We were saddened when we heard that he lost his battle with cancer. I hesitated to tell Katie and couldn't find the words to tell her. She didn't say much and kept her feelings about his death inside. She had just started her butt-kicking chemo and was feeling puny. However, she insisted that we go to the funeral to support Brooke. Wes and I loaded Katie and the wheelchair up in the truck. We were extremely late getting there but decided to go anyway. I'm glad we did, because Brooke and Katie were so glad to see each other.

CLEAN HOUSE

Katie was extremely weak on the butt-kicking chemo. These were much longer stays in the hospital than before—not to mention, she was only a few weeks out of knee surgery. Her counts were extremely low at times, which meant we all had to wear masks, including her. Before she could even go home, the house would have to be completely sanitized and all my plants moved outside. Her grandparents, Mary Alice and Ralph, offered to come up and clean my entire house. I was thankful, because Mary Alice was excellent at this, and I knew I wouldn't have to worry if it would be done right.

Katie was glad to see her grandparents. They went to clinic with us the next day. When we got there, Katie needed a transfusion, because her counts were so low. When Ralph saw her lying there with all the tubes and blood bags, he broke down and started crying. By now, I was so used to it that I had forgotten how distressing this could be for someone seeing it for the first time. Katie finished up, we went home, and Mary Alice and Ralph left the next day. ♣

CHAPTER 12

PLEASE, GOD, NOT ER!

A few days after her grandparents left, I was in my pajamas about to go to bed when I decided I'd better go check on Katie and make sure she wasn't running any fever. My heart sank when I read 101° on the thermometer.

No, Lord, please, not tonight! All I want to do is go to bed.

I was so tired. Katie was exhausted, too, and still in pain. She begged me to not take her in, but we had no choice. This could be life-threatening, and we couldn't ignore the high fever.

We got to the hospital right before midnight. When we walked in, ER was filled with so many parents and screaming kids that there was no place to even sit. There were no beds available on the eighth or ninth floor for cancer patients, so they put us in a holding room to keep Katie isolated. I was afraid for her to even breathe in that place. We stayed there two hours, until they moved us to an examining room in ER. Katie got in the bed, I took the rocking chair, and Wes sat in her wheelchair. They gave Katie a transfusion, because her hemoglobin was so low, but they didn't start her antibiotics until four hours into our visit.

"God, *please* let a room open up!" I cried out of frustration.

Wes was bent over the foot of Katie's bed trying to get comfortable. My back hurt, and I longed to be in my own bed. There were screaming babies outside our door who never let up. We felt like we were in hell.

Wes and I slept about 30 minutes that night, and Katie slept maybe a little more. Wes left at 4:00 p.m. the next day to pick up Bethany from school and came back a few hours later with food and toiletries. I hadn't washed my face or brushed my teeth for almost 24 hours.

The following night, we were still in ER waiting for a hospital room. Wes left at 9:00 p.m. to go home. Katie and I watched Jack Frost and fell asleep around 10:00 p.m. but were awakened at 1:30 a.m. to go to the ninth floor. Finally, after 26 hours of being in ER, with two and a half hours of sleep in two days, the elevator door opened to the ninth floor.

Right on cue, Katie threw up. She hated the ninth floor.

GETTING TOWED

The following day after Wes got off work, he brought us some food, because Katie and I were both so tired of hospital food. Instead of valet parking, he decided to park at the Wells Fargo bank across the street, because he needed to get cash. He wanted to bring Katie her food first and then go back and get the cash. Wes saw a man watching him who was getting into his car, but he didn't think much of it.

The bank closed at 6:00 p.m. It was around 6:00 p.m. There were towing signs everywhere, but Wes thought since we he was coming back to get cash later, and it was closing time anyway, that it would be alright to leave the car there, right? Wrong! When he left that night at 10:30, someone (probably that man) had called the towing company and had our car impounded. That meant I had to get dressed, leave Katie alone in the hospital, find the towing place, and take him there. It cost us $103.00, and that was a lot of money at the time. It was also over an hour to drive home for Wes. I got back to Katie's room well after midnight. We had been customers of Wells Fargo for many years and probably could have fought it, but neither one of us had the energy for it.

Katie finally finished up all three rounds of the butt-kicking chemo. It was the day we looked forward to for so long. The doctor came with her thawed-out platelets. It made her cold when they transfused them back into her body, so they wrapped her in a blanket. It only took 45 minutes, and she was so excited about her last round of chemo, she wanted me to take her for a spin around the hospital in her wheelchair.

Ashley said she was the easiest patient she ever had. We would miss Ashley. One of the nurses made a big celebration banner for Katie's last day, and all the staff signed it. Everyone on duty came by to congratulate Katie on finishing her last chemo treatment. We stayed one more night. Her counts were high enough the next day, so we got to go home. We were all elated.

Weee, I'm done with all my chemo treatments! Yay! Tomorrow I get my braces back on (yuck). Good thing I still have that Vicodin tho, right? Hehe, I might get to go to Japan for my Make-A-Wish. Yay, hopefully, I'll get a lesson from a real artist. Physical therapy is still a pain in the butt, (or should I say knee?) Can't wait till I can walk again. I'm tired. Mom would kill me if she knew I was up this late.

KATIE'S JOURNAL ENTRY, MARCH 17, 2002

JESUS WITH SKIN ON

Katie was 5'6" tall and had dropped down to 94 pounds. She just didn't have an appetite. Her diet consisted of two crackers a day and only a little water. I tried everything to get her to eat to no avail. Even the nutritionist at the hospital was concerned. By now, she was hairless and brow-less with no thick, long eyelashes left. She sat slumped in her wheelchair most of the time. She looked like she had just come out of a concentration camp. I tried to ignore most of the stares by focusing my attention on Katie.

However, one day in particular really got to me. We had a check-up that day, and, afterwards, we were outside the hospital waiting for the valet to bring our car around. I saw a lady looking at Katie with this horrified look on her face. I heard her gasp.

I wanted to scream at her, "Stop looking at my child like that! She's not a freak!" I really wanted to clobber that woman. I was so glad Katie didn't see her. We were at a hospital for sick children, for heaven's sake!

On another occasion, we had gone out to eat with the whole family, and I guess the waiter was uncomfortable around Katie.

He wouldn't make eye contact with her, and, when it came time for her to order, he looked at me and said pointing to Katie, "What would he like to order?"

I was irritated and said, "*He* is a she, and *she* would like the grilled chicken."

The positives far outweighed the negatives, though. Another time, we were outside the hospital waiting for the valet to bring our car around. A woman came up to me nonchalantly and asked if her daughter could give her toy to Katie.

"Yes, of course," I said.

The daughter, about five years of age, smiled at Katie and said, "Here, I hope this makes you feel better." She handed Katie her well-loved stuffed kitten and skipped off.

Neither one of them were making a big deal of it, but it made a huge impact on the both of us. I was so overwhelmed, I could hardly choke out a thank you. Katie smiled for the first time in a long time and was very touched by the little girl's kindness. She held onto the kitten all the way home and even slept with it that night.

I asked the Lord for a special blessing on those kind strangers. I wondered why more people couldn't be like that. That was Jesus with skin on.

How I appreciated the clerk who would smile and talk to Katie like a normal person. We were in Claire's at the mall one time, and Katie was still in her wheelchair. She and the clerk must've talked for 30 minutes. I know Katie was lonely during this time, since her friends were all in school and she was usually at the clinic, at the hospital, or had to be isolated at home. Katie was a people person. Not having her friends around was one of the hardest things she dealt with. It was a very lonely time for us both.

I learned something in all the different situations I experienced with people during this time. People with disabilities are just normal people and want to be treated as normal people. I didn't like it when someone ignored my daughter or treated her as if she didn't have a brain with which to think. It reminded me of 1 Samuel 16:7:

> *But the LORD said to Samuel,* "Don't judge by his appearance or height, for I have rejected him. The LORD doesn't see things the way you see them. People judge by outward appearance, but the LORD looks at the heart." (NLT)

Another time, we were at the clinic, and we saw a bunch of people passing us.

My friend, Elayne, saw him first and said, "There's Craig

Biggio!"

I wondered what he was doing at the hospital, and then someone told me about his Sunshine Kids Foundation for children with
serious ailments. Now, I'm not really an Astros fan, but I am a Craig
Biggio fan. I watched him crawl into the back of a Suburban to talk
with a very sick little boy who was too weak to get out of his vehicle.
No fanfare, no cameras, no big deal—but it made a huge impact on
all of us. That was Jesus with skin on.

We saw so many acts of kindness around us and experienced
many ourselves. Most of the time, people were doing it for the right
reasons by alleviating someone else's pain and not trying to make
themselves feel better. ♦

CHAPTER 13

GOOD NEWS AND
A VERY BAD DAY

Even though Katie was through with chemo, she still had to go back to the clinic two or three times a week for blood counts, MRIs, and all the other tests she had before chemo. In March, we got the wonderful news that the cancer looked like it was all gone. The scans were clear. We were all so relieved.

We decided to have Katie's braces put back on and start moving towards getting her back into the swing of things. She was out of the wheelchair now, too, and started to put some weight back on. She was able to start hanging out with her friends again, and it helped her feel normal for the first time in a very long time. We were so grateful to God for giving us our lives back—or, so we thought.

After the latest scan in May, Melody came in with the results.

She took a deep breath and said, "The scans came back with two spots. Each one is about an inch in size on her right lung. It has metastasized, and we need to discuss what our next course of action will be. It's acting very aggressive. We can do more chemo, and Katie would have a 50/50 chance of survival."

We were stunned. Katie seemed so strong, healthy, and in such good spirits again. Katie and I both burst into tears. I reached over and hugged her for a long time.

Katie caught her breath, and, through her sobs, she said, "Mom, I don't want any more chemo."

I felt like I'd been kicked in the stomach. "I know, honey," I told her. "You're mature enough to make that decision, but let's at least pray about it and talk it over with Dad."

Melody listened politely to our conversation. She didn't try to persuade Katie into doing more chemo. She also mentioned something about Katie's quality of life. Anyway, we were still sure God was going to heal her.

Katie did go through the surgery to remove the two tumors in her right lung. It was a painful surgery with a four-day hospital stay, but the surgeon said the tumors looked contained. He also said the x-rays looked as though she never had surgery. We were still hopeful.

I'm in pain, always in pain. If it's not one thing, it's another. I'm so sick of being in pain. One day, it'll stop. But, Lord, I thought I was done. Please, I want to stop now. Why can't I be normal? I don't want to go through this anymore. I'm tired.

Why did the cancer come back? Why?? I hate you cancer!! I hate you! You ruined my life! I want to be done. I don't want to go through chemotherapy again. I want to be done.

Why do I have to worry about dying at such a young age? I should only be worrying about acne and guys. People say I'm strong, that I have so much courage. But, why? Why do they think that? I'm just a small 15-year-old limping along through this cold world.

Lord, please heal me. I believe You have healed me already. But, I pray to You tonight, please, please don't let me go through chemotherapy. Amen.

KATIE'S JOURNAL ENTRY, MAY 30, 2002

He answered that prayer. ♣

CHAPTER 14

MAKE-A-WISH

After we got the bad news about the spots on her lung, Dr. Marali insisted Katie take advantage of Make-A-Wish. I think, in his mind, her chances didn't look good. Dr. Marali asked Katie what she would want if she could have anything, and she didn't hesitate.

"I want to go to Japan and meet Toshihiro Kawamoto, the animator who draws *Cowboy Bebop*."

I thought to myself, *No, Katie, tell them you want to go to Hawaii!*

Wes and I were not too thrilled with Japan. It just wasn't at the top of our favorite places to visit. But, for some reason, Katie was enamored with it because of all the anime she loved drawing. I got a call the next day from the Make-A-Wish representative. She asked what Katie wanted, and I told her she wanted to meet the famous animator from Japan.

She said, "I'm not sure we can make that wish happen. No one has ever requested that before. I don't have any contacts there, and I don't know how to go about it."

"Can I try contacting the studio myself?" I asked.

She was hesitant. "I guess it wouldn't hurt to try."

I could tell she didn't have much hope of me getting anywhere, but, because my daughter wanted it, I was determined to make it happen. So, I got one of the *Cowboy Bebop* VHS tapes and saw Sunrise Studios on the back with an email address. I knew it was a long shot, but I explained Katie's situation in the email and told them all about Make-A-Wish.

I was so excited to hear back from them the next day. I could tell their English wasn't very good, but they were agreeable and even asked if Katie would like to have a private drawing lesson with Toshihiro Kawamoto! She was so excited.

We were a little concerned about the extra finances it would take for all of us to go when we found out Make a Wish wouldn't cover Nick since he was of college age. We knew we didn't have the money. Cancer is an expensive disease, even with insurance. There were so many hidden costs, and, if Katie needed or wanted something, we did everything in our financial power to get it for her.

Bethany knew it, too, and would secretly tell Katie to ask Mom and Dad for something she wanted. One day, I started getting suspicious when Katie asked for some high-end mascara (she didn't have eyelashes). When I asked her why she wanted that, she confessed that she didn't want it and Bethany had put her up to it. Parents will do anything for their child who has cancer—at least, the parents I know.

JAPAN

We were still trying to figure out a way to have Nick go on the trip with us. It was important for us to have the whole family go—especially Nick, since he was the one who had gotten Katie started on anime.

When people found out about our trip, donations started pouring in. It was enough to cover Nick's expenses with enough left over for some spending money. The Lord was so gracious to us!

I called Make-A-Wish back and gave them Sunrise Studio's contact information so they could confirm everything. I found out later that my email went to the San Francisco office, and they translated it into Japanese and forwarded it to the headquarters in Japan. It took a lot of hoops to jump through, but when God opens the door, there isn't any shutting it. I'm so thankful they were agreeable. When it came time for our trip, a limo was sent to the house to take us to the airport. It was a 12-hour flight there. We flew coach, and that was a long time for Katie to sit like a pretzel.

When we got to Tokyo, the first thing we noticed was how much taller we were than the Japanese. Both my husband and son are 6'4" tall and looked like Amazons compared to them. The World Cup was playing in Japan while we were there, and people from literally all over the world were in our hotel or on the bullet trains we were riding. We loved seeing the different people and all the dialects interacting with each other.

HER LESSONS

Katie was scheduled for her anime lessons the next day. Mr. Watanabe, our contact, made the hour-long bus ride to our hotel to meet us and escorted us to the other side of Tokyo at Sunrise Studios. I appreciated him for making sure we found our way to the studio. When we got there, it was a small studio and we met our English-speaking Japanese interpreter who would be with us the whole time. We met the owner of the studio who presented Katie with a silkscreen picture of the main character in *Cowboy Bebop*.

After the tour of the studio, Katie met another animator, lesser-known than Toshihiro Kawamoto. He was an animator for the series Gundham Wing and also wanted to give Katie a lesson. She sat shyly next to him and spoke little and softly. Through the interpreter, he instructed her on animation. At first, she was a little embarrassed to be drawing in front of the experts, but he gave her some pointers and she felt more at ease.

Next, she finally got to meet the famous animator for *Cowboy Bebop*, Toshihiro Kawamoto. He was like a rock star to her. They sat down together, and he drew several pictures, signed them, and gave them to her. Then, he asked her to draw one for him and sign her name. It was a sweet moment, one that I wish we could have freeze framed. She was so content, so happy, like she belonged there.

The famous animator left for a little while and came back with all these original art works that he had done for *Cowboy Bebop*. He gave them to Katie. They were progression drawings from the anime series. We were all in awe of the graciousness and generosity shown to us and especially Katie. It was a dream come true for her, and I will always be thankful to the Make-A-Wish Foundation and Sunrise Studios for our trip to Japan.

> I was so selfish at the end of 8th grade. I was re-reading my journal, and I came across a section where the doctors said I had a stress fracture. "God better have a good reason for this." That's what I said. Aarg! Stupid, selfish little girl! Can't you realize that all God's plans work out for the best?? Yes, I had cancer. And yes, it came back. But now I will have an amazing testimony of how God has healed me and given me better health than before. God must have something great planned for my life or else why would the devil keep targeting me out of the family? It is because of cancer that I have been able to do all these great things. It changed my life. Now I trust God and believe in Him even more than I have before. The more the devil tries to get me down, the better my testimony of healness becomes.

KATIE'S JOURNAL ENTRY, JUNE 25, 2001

CHAPTER 15

TROUBLE BREATHING

In August, we enrolled Katie in the public high school close to our home. It was a big school, and she had trouble navigating it. She was trying to hurry to class so she wouldn't be late again and fell down six steps. Her appetite was also starting to wane. She ended up attending school only five days.

She started getting wheezy and choked easily. She would spit up blood occasionally and was running a low grade fever. Her latest CT chest scan revealed fluid on her right lung, but Dr. Marali wasn't exactly sure what it was. He said he couldn't get a clear view of the lung but scheduled surgery for the next day to remove the fluid. The surgeon removed four ounces of fluid but still couldn't tell what it was. He also said her right lung was partially collapsed at the bottom. Several days later, Dr. Marali told us that the fluid didn't have any cancer cells in it, which we were very happy about. It also tested negative for pneumonia, but he thought it was still some type of infection. Katie was also experiencing a lot of pain in her back, stomach, and shoulder.

CLINIC VISIT TURNS INTO ER

Katie was scheduled for another x-ray. Elayne went with us, and I was so glad to have her there. After the x-ray, Melody wanted to see Katie, so we headed over to the clinic. Katie was still wheezing, so Melody listened to her chest and hooked her up to an instrument that checks oxygen levels.

All of a sudden, everyone started rushing around. Her oxygen levels were critically low, so they hurriedly put her on oxygen. While the nurses were tending to Katie, Melody and Dr. Mueller, another child cancer doctor, escorted Elayne and I into a conference room with the door shut.

Dr. Mueller looked at me very solemnly and said, "We have a very serious situation. The tumor has spread all over her chest in one week's time. It's closing off her trachea and choking her to death. By looking at her scans, we can tell something else is growing in the abdomen and behind her knee." Dr. Mueller stopped, looked me in the eye, and said, "She can get the stuff she's been coughing up stuck in her airways and die anytime. She could have died at home the last night from all the terrible coughing. Unless we do emergency surgery, she has only 24 to 48 hours to live."

Elayne totally lost it. She began sobbing. I sat there about to puke, in total disbelief. Everything started going into slow motion. Elayne began pulling herself together and started calling people to pray. I told her to call my friend, Cheryl Wheeler, who then called Duncan and Laurie Dodds. Wes and I met them once at a volleyball game. Our daughters were friends, but we barely knew them. But, I knew they would be faithful to pray.

We went back to the room where Katie was hooked up to oxygen. The nurses quickly placed her on a gurney.

With urgency in her voice, Melody said, "We've got to get her to ER right now!"

As we were all racing down the hallway, I looked at Melody and said, "Whether my child lives or dies, my faith in Jesus will never fail me!" I don't even know why I said that the way I did, but, later, I would actually see that come to pass.

While I was running alongside Katie, I heard the Lord's voice say to me, *Do you trust Me, no matter what?*

I said out loud, "Yes, Lord, I trust You no matter what!" I quickly answered Him, because I just knew that He was going to heal my daughter. I called Wes at work, and he met us in ER.

FAITH OF A CHILD

Katie was calm during all the commotion happening around her. The pulmonary and heart doctors examined Katie first and then met with us outside her room. They told us that the cancer had almost completely closed off her trachea, and the airway only had an opening the size of a pencil for her to breathe through. We were told of all the risks involved with surgery, and we needed to make a decision right now on what to do. How was I going to tell her, my youngest child, that she only had a day—maybe two—to live?

I choked back tears, swallowed hard, and leaned into her bed. "Katie, the doctors are saying that you only have 24 to 48 hours to live. Right now, our only option is emergency surgery to open up your trachea."

She calmly said, "Let's do surgery, then."

"Well, the only thing is, Katie, it's extremely dangerous, and there's no guarantee you'll even pull through," I said.

She said bravely, "Well, I don't want it, then." Before we left her bedside to let the surgeons know our decision, Katie looked at me and her dad and said, "This is just an opportunity for God to do a greater miracle."

"You're exactly right, Katie," I said, and I thought to myself, *Here, my child is on her death bed, and she's proclaiming God's miracles.* When she said that, it gave me the courage to face what was happening head on.

DODIE OSTEEN

That night, Katie's breathing stabilized enough to move her to ICU. We had more than 100 concerned people showing their support for our family in ICU. Bethany's volleyball team and parents, Nick and his law school friends, and our friends and extended family. When Duncan and Laurie Dodds showed up, we asked Duncan to pray for Katie. There were ten of us gathered around Katie's bed to pray in ICU, but I thought, Man, I sure wish Dodie Osteen were here to pray. God had healed Dodie of liver cancer in 1982, and, to this day, she is still cancer-free.

Somehow Dodie had gotten word about Katie, and when I looked up, I couldn't believe my eyes! Like the parting of the Red Sea, Dodie made her way through the crowd toward us.

She smiled, hugged us warmly, and said, "I remember you!" (That was amazing, since we only had a brief conversation before.)

We gathered around Katie's bed, and Dodie began to pray with such confidence and authority, I could feel the hairs on my arms standing up! We found her to be the closest thing to Jesus we had ever seen. She was so kind and loving.

I showed Dodie my notepad with all the healing scriptures that I spoke over Katie every day.

She took the pad from me, pointed it downward, and said boldly, "You see this, devil? We confess that Katie is healed and you are defeated!" Then, she held it up to heaven and said, "My Father, this is her mother's confession, and her parents believe that your word is true!"

When she was through praying, she bent over to give Katie a kiss but couldn't reach her. She asked Duncan to give her a boost, and she leaned over and gave Katie a kiss on the forehead. We were all in awe at what we had witnessed that night watching this small frame of a woman kick the devil in the teeth.

ICU

ICU is not a place you would want to camp out for very long. Since there were no sofa beds or lounge chairs in Katie's room, if we wanted to get any rest, it would be in the main waiting area of ICU, which consisted of recliners lining each of the four walls. Bethany had a game earlier, so a few of her teammates and coaches stayed until 4:00 a.m. with her in the waiting area, and then left.

Wes was in Katie's room in the rocking chair dozing off and on. Elayne, Bethany, and I found a room off to the side of the waiting area and slept a few hours on the floor without pillows or blankets. After a few hours of trying to sleep, I looked over at Bethany and noticed she still had her knee pads pulled up over her knees.

The next day, another steady stream of well-wishers began showing up. It was exhausting talking to everyone. My body ached for sleep. I felt as though I'd been beaten with a baseball bat.

STILL BELIEVING GOD

After very little sleep, Melody and another oncologist I didn't know wanted to meet with Wes and me privately. This doctor began describing what the end of Katie's life was going to be like. Fear shot through me. I felt the nausea coming back, and, this time, the room began to spin on me. They said that Katie would be gasping for air, clutching the sheets, and flailing around in bed.

I let them finish, and then I looked Melody straight in the eyes and declared, "We are still believing God for a miracle!"

"I hope you get it," she said.

I know they were trying to prepare me, but I had to keep telling myself that all was well and God was still in control. ♦

Katie, age 6

Nick, age 17, Bethany, age 10, Katie, age 9

Katie and Brooke "monkeying around"

Katie's last July 4th, 2002

Katie's 8th grade graduation

Katie's last July 4th, 2002

Getting fresh air
after knee surgery

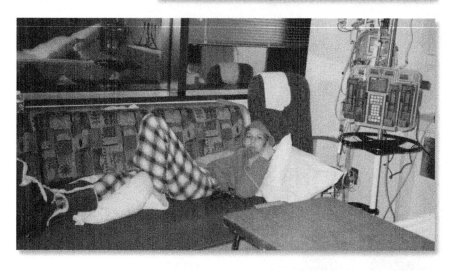

Katie's last
Christmas, 2001

No more chemo!

Make-A-Wish trip and private lesson with Toshihiro Kawamoto

Make-A-Wish trip

CHAPTER 16

THE ELEVENTH FLOOR

After three long days of ICU, the staff didn't know what to do with Katie. She had already surpassed everyone's expectations, and we had so many visitors, the other parents began complaining about all the noise our people were making. They decided to move Katie into a room of her own and asked her which floor she wanted to recover on, knowing she could die any second.

She didn't hesitate and immediately said the eleventh floor. It was the surgery recovery floor she had been on after her knee replacement and was much quieter than the cancer floor. And it didn't make her vomit.

I found out later that the nurses were freaked out about having to take care of a dying cancer patient on their floor. Somehow, the head nurse gave the okay, so they moved Katie up to the eleventh floor. When we got there, the head nurse introduced herself. She knew we were believers and asked if she could pray for Katie. I have never in my life heard anyone pray like that before, except Dodie Osteen. She also mentioned that once they got word that Katie was coming, they had gathered around and prayed for her before she had even gotten there.

After the head nurse left the room, Katie looked at me and said, "Wow, that was a powerful prayer!"

DOING BETTER

For 36 hours, none of us had brushed our teeth, slept, taken a shower, or eaten much, and we were all so relieved to be able to do that again. I was begging for people to go home, so we could all get some rest. Dr. Marali told us we could go home with some assistance (hospice care) if we wanted to. We decided to stay.

No one was expecting her to live very long, but four days after being moved up to the eleventh floor, her breathing became normal, and her O2 levels were at 100! Her appetite picked up, and she began eating normally again. She was in good spirits and began drawing more.

Wes told Dr. Marali that we were expecting a miracle and his response was, "Absolutely!" But, he went on to say that it was the steroid that was helping her breathe normally again. He said she still had some restriction in her right lung. However, he failed to mention that the week before it wasn't even inflating. Wes said the first night in ICU, her right side wasn't rising when she breathed in, but now we could see that it was. The doctors explained away the improvement, but we sure didn't. We just knew God was healing her. Dr. Bertuch was the cancer doctor on call and came by to check on Katie. She asked Katie how she was doing, and Katie said emphatically, "A lot better than the doctors say!"

Everyone burst out laughing. It was a classic moment.

DR. DEATH AND THE DRUGS

I don't know who this doctor was. He was a resident doctor making his rounds that day. When he came into our room, he never once asked Katie how she was doing.

"When the end comes, we have morphine ready to be used at a moment's notice," he said. "It will make it easier for your daughter."

"My daughter heard everything you just said," I responded. "So, thank you for your time. You may leave now."

From that day on, we did not allow that doctor back in the room with Katie. After a while, I'm sure he caught on to our excuses that Katie was always in the bathroom or sleeping. We referred to him as Dr. Death.

PEACE

One of the things people would always say when they came into our room was how peaceful it was. Duncan Dodds had given us a new CD that Cindy Cruse-Ratcliff had just released, and we played it non-stop. It helped keep our focus on the Lord, and we sensed God's presence as we played it. We never stopped playing it. If it would finish in the middle of the night, I would get up and hit play on the boom box.

I had gotten to know the charge nurse on that floor, Kathy, pretty well. She must've been having a rough day. She busted through the door, shut it behind her, leaned her head back, and closed her eyes. Nobody said a word. Katie and I just sat there watching her for the longest time.

Finally, she looked over at me and said, "I came in here to get some peace." I thought it was ironic that our daughter was there fighting for her life, and stressed-out nurses were coming into our room to find peace.

CONSUELO

We met Consuelo a few days after we got to the eleventh floor. All the nurses we had so far had been very engaging, but not Consuelo. She worked the night shift and was all business. She didn't smile, make eye contact, or say a word, except to ask Katie about how she was feeling and if she needed anything.

This routine went on for a couple of nights, until she happened to be taking Katie's blood pressure when the song "There is a Fountain" was playing on our boom box. This song was done partly in Spanish, and when she heard the word *consuelo*—the same word as her name—she cocked her head to the side and started listening to the words.

I saw my opportunity to break the ice, so I asked her, "What does

Consuelo mean?"

"Consolation," she said softly. "like comforting someone."

"That's a good name," I said. She didn't respond.

The next night, she and Katie woke me up talking in the middle of the night. There were many such nights. Consuelo was indeed a comfort to Katie, and they became such good friends. Consuelo proved to be one of the most dedicated nurses we had in our 16 months at Texas Children's.

KATIE GETS STRONGER

Two weeks after Katie was admitted to ICU, she showed such improvement. Friends would stop by and visit and couldn't believe how healthy she looked and acted. Even the doctors were scratching their heads. One night, Elayne, Jim, Wes, and I were hanging outside her room eating and talking.

Katie hopped out of bed, opened the door, and yelled, "Hey, I'm in here by myself!"

We paused, looked over, and saw Katie in her hospital gown holding her IV pole. We all started laughing.

BREATHING BETTER

The next morning, the lung doctor came by to listen to Katie's breathing and was amazed at how much airflow she had. Katie told him that she was going to walk out of this hospital healed. The lung doctor said they must pray to the same God. He said that when she was admitted to ER two weeks previously, she only had an opening the size of a pencil in her windpipe. Now, it sounded like she had about a 1 ½" opening. He said he didn't know that for sure without an x-ray, but she definitely had a lot more breathing room.

Later, Dr. Bertuch came by and said she spoke to the lung doctor but wanted to hear for herself how much airflow Katie had. She leaned down to listen and was smiling.

She said, "I didn't believe it when he told me how much airflow she was getting. I listened this morning and didn't hear airflow like that! That's amazing!"

Every nurse who listened to Katie said the same thing. It was very encouraging, but, later that evening, Katie started running a 101° fever. ♣

CHAPTER 17

HER DREAMS

Katie began having bad dreams. She would wake up in the middle of the night very frightened. She had grown attached to Duncan and asked me to call him so he could pray over her dreams. Sometimes, he and Laurie would make a surprise visit to the hospital in the morning before work, and he would pray for her then. She had a lot of confidence in his prayers.

One morning, she asked for him again, but I knew he was in an important meeting with Integrity Records and told her I would call him later when he got out. She kept insisting I call him now. I told her no. She asked me again, pleading with me. I finally gave in and hesitantly dialed his number.

He answered and said, "I was just talking about you guys! I was telling the executive producer here at Integrity how much that CD has ministered to your family. How's my girl this morning?"

I apologized profusely for bothering him and told him she insisted I call him and have him pray over her dreams. I handed her the phone, and he prayed for her. After that, she began having dreams of a spiritual nature. She had a dream the next night that gave her so much peace, though it really unsettled me.

"Oh, Mom, I had the best dream last night," Katie said early the next morning. Even before I had my coffee, I was so excited to hear about it.

I asked, "What was it?"

"I dreamt I was at a Bible study at church with all my friends," she said. "I was being disruptive, and my friends kept telling me to be quiet. I didn't listen and kept on talking.

"Someone said, 'The Teacher's coming.'

"When I looked up, I saw Jesus walking up the aisle toward me. He was this clear gold color.

"I cried out, 'Oh, Jesus! I'm so sorry!' and put my head down on the pew.

"Then, He chuckled and said to me, 'Oh, Katie,' and touched me on the head."

Katie closed her eyes, leaned her head back on the pillow, and smiled. "Mom, when Jesus touched me, I turned this clear gold color, too. But, none of my other friends turned that color. I felt so good. If that's what heaven is like, I'm ready to go right now."

I protested and told Katie it wasn't her time, that I needed her here on earth with me. She had this dreamy look in her eyes. No matter how much I pleaded with her, she was not convinced that life on earth was better than heaven.

I knew she was right, but it kicked my selfishness in the teeth. Surely God would not require me to give up my child so early in life.

How I wrestled with that. I felt this huge war going on inside me. I fought so hard, prayed constantly, read more healing scriptures out loud than ever, and began to praise Jesus even more. I didn't care who was around. I knew God could turn things around in an instant. I knew He had the power to do that, and I kept declaring out loud that my daughter was healed no matter who was around. I did everything I knew to do, including fasting, to move God's hand. We were still expecting a miracle.

Believing nurses and doctors agreed with us, but Melody had her concerns. She stopped by Katie's room while on her break at the clinic. She asked if she could talk to me outside.

I shut the door behind us, and she said to me, "Valerie, I'm concerned you're putting too much stock in all this miracle stuff."

"What do you mean?" I responded. It caught me off guard, especially since she had never questioned my faith in the 16 months I had known her.

She continued, "There's no guarantee that God is going to heal Katie, and, if He doesn't, I don't want you to be disappointed."

"Melody, you're absolutely right," I said. "I have no guarantee my child is going to live. But, one thing I do know is my faith in Jesus will not fail me." It was kind of an odd way of putting it, like the day we were rushing Katie on a gurney down to ER when I told Melody the same exact thing. I wanted her to know that I meant every word. I wanted her to know that I wasn't letting go of Jesus, and I knew for sure He wasn't letting go of me.

Who else did I have? The closest person to me was my husband, and he had failed me many times, just like I had failed him. But, I knew Jesus would never fail me. I held onto Him tighter than ever.

I just recently made the connection in scripture where Jesus prayed for Peter the night before He was crucified. Peter would deny Him three times, even though he said he never would. In Luke 22:32, Jesus said to Peter, "But I have prayed for you, that your faith should not fail; and when you have returned to me, strengthen your brothers." I believe Jesus prays for us even now so we don't lose our faith in Him.

Jesus also instructed Peter to strengthen his brothers. I believe He tells me often to do the same. ◆

CHAPTER 18

GROWING OLD AND THINKING ABOUT LEAVING

K atie and I had some of the best conversations in the hospital. We talked about everything. We would reminisce about funny childhood stories, usually involving her and her sister getting into trouble. We loved laughing about old times. Not a day passed that we weren't telling each other "I love you." She also told me that had she not gotten cancer, she probably wouldn't be serving God. She wasn't in a good place the year before she was diagnosed. Somehow, I knew she was right, and that was a hard pill to swallow.

Serious illnesses have a way of growing children up before their time, too. Many are robbed of just being kids. Katie was no exception. During her cancer treatment, she would converse with the doctors and nurses like a grown woman. I quit answering questions that she could easily answer herself. She had become so wise, it was like talking to an 80-year-old woman who had learned and experienced so much about life. One day, a fringe friend wanted to bring some other friends to the hospital who Katie didn't know and she really wasn't up for visitors.

She told me, "I don't want to be anybody's field trip."

KATIE'S REQUEST

While we were stuck in the hospital, life didn't slow down for Katie's sister, Bethany. Her high school volleyball team won district and was hoping for a state playoff run. Bethany had come by to see Katie in the hospital after practice late one evening.

Katie had missed her whole season and told her, "Win state for me, Bethany." Katie knew what a big deal it was for her and the rest of the team.

THINKING ABOUT LEAVING

Three weeks after Katie was admitted to the hospital, she was particularly quiet. I was reading and looked up to see her staring intently out the window past me. She was so deep in thought, she didn't notice me looking at her.

Finally, I asked, "What are you thinking about, Katie?"

Her face softened when I interrupted her stare. She looked at me, smiled, and shook her head no. I asked her again, and she said softly, "Nothing."

I knew deep down she was thinking about something that would upset me. I'm still not exactly sure, but, after that day, she became more introspective.

Several hours later, I was catching up on some reading.

Katie looked over at me and said, "Thank you, Mom."

"For what?" I asked.

"For everything you've done for me," she said. "I can't imagine going through all this without you here."

I said, "Honey, I have no regrets and would do it all over again if I had to."

"I know you would," she said softly.

2 CORINTHIANS 4:16

The next morning when I woke up, Katie looked over at me and said, "The Lord gave me a scripture last night. I scratched it onto my Styrofoam cup with my gel pen."

I was so excited. I just knew that God had spoken to my daughter. "What is it, Katie?"

"2 Corinthians 4:16."

I hurriedly opened the Bible and read, T*hat is why we never give up.*

"Yes, Lord!" I said. "We won't *ever* give up!"

Then, I continued reading the rest of the scripture. *Though our bodies are dying—*

"Dying? NO! Katie, I don't really like that scripture," I told her. "You must've heard wrong; it has the word dying in it." I thought, *No, Lord, that can't be right!*

I finished reading it:…*our spirits are being renewed.*

We went ahead and added it to our daily reading, except Wes changed the word dying to weak. We added verses 15, 17, and 18. In the New Living Translation, it reads:

All this is for your benefit. And as God's grace reaches more and more people, there will be great thanksgiving, and God will re-

ceive more and more glory. That is why we never give up. Though our bodies are dying, our spirits are being renewed every day. For our present troubles won't last very long. Yet they produce for us a glory that vastly outweighs them and will last forever! So we don't look at the troubles we can see now; rather, we fix our gaze on things that cannot be seen. For the things we see now will soon be gone, but the things we cannot see will last forever.

I believe God gave this to Katie for what was ahead.

OUR ASSIGNMENT

We read healing scriptures out loud several times a day. We felt it was important what we were allowing in her hospital room. We never turned the TV on and only listened to the praise and worship CD that Duncan had given us. When he found out people were asking about it, he gave us ten copies to share with those around us. For about three weeks, we were deliberate in who we gave them to. I would pray over each one, and I believe some of those CDs went to people who were maybe on the fence and not really sure of their salvation or weak in their faith. Some went to nurses and other patients, but it was the last CD that I remember most.

One day, a young janitor was sweeping our room with his big duster. We had the CD playing, and Katie and I both noticed the young man was lost in the music. He just kept sweeping slowly back and forth. Katie cut her eyes over at me and smiled.

Finally, the young man looked up and said, "I just love choral music."

"Here," I said, reaching over and grabbing the last one off the shelf. "I want you to have this."

You would've thought I had given him a million dollars. He said with a smile, "Thank you so much, ma'am," and walked out of the room. Our assignment of evangelizing the eleventh floor was done.

CHAPTER 19

IT WASN'T UP TO ME

When Katie woke up Friday morning, her breathing was a lot more labored. Consuelo had worked the night before and was supposed to get off work at 7:00 that morning. When she saw Katie was having trouble breathing, she told me she was going to work another shift so she could keep an eye on her. Debbie Schultz called and wanted to come see Katie and asked what she wanted for lunch. Katie requested her favorite food, turkey and dressing. She barely picked at it. Debbie stayed most of the afternoon and left. Wes arrived at the hospital around 5:30.

Dr. Marali took one look at Katie and wanted to know how long she had been having trouble breathing. He ordered the pulmonary doctor up right away to check her out and put her on oxygen. They gave her a steroid shot to open up her airways. Her heart began racing, and her oxygen levels were dropping. That day started out peaceful but became mayhem in just a few minutes.

I called Debbie on her cell phone. "You'd better get back up here! Katie's taken a turn for the worse, and I need people here who'll pray!"

She quickly made a U-turn and headed back to the hospital. I called my friends Jim and Elayne Slater, and they came busting through the door soon after. I also called Cheryl Wheeler and Duncan and Laurie Dodds to come pray for Katie. Katie's vitals began to stabilize. Duncan and Laurie left around 10 o'clock, and Cheryl left around midnight, all feeling confident that Katie was going to be okay.

After they left, Jim, Elayne, Debbie, Wes, and I began to sing praise and worship. We were all on our knees, hands lifted in worship, believing God for a miracle. At one point, I looked up and saw Katie with her hands lifted up to Jesus, too. It was an awesome sight to see my 15-year-old daughter in total submission to the Father. God's presence was tangible—you could feel it, and peace swept over us.

Wes was sitting by her right side stroking her arm. I was on her other side, and she would squeeze my hand every so often. Her O2 levels began to normalize, her heart quit racing, and her blood pressure leveled out. This was at about 2 o'clock in the morning. We were watching our miracle unfold before our eyes!

Katie lifted the oxygen mask and asked, "Where's the tall man?"

We were baffled. "Who are you talking about Katie?" I asked.

"The tall man," she repeated.

Tall man? Did she mean Duncan, who stood about 6'5"? No, she probably would have called him by name. Some might think she was hallucinating because of the drugs she was on, but there was no other indication of her seeing things or talking weird.

We are convinced it was an angel only she could see. The reason I say that is because a few years later when Katie's grandfather, Ralph, was dying, Mary Alice, Wes, and I were standing around his bed. He was diagnosed with Alzheimer's and was not very lucid his last few days. He was a farmer all his life, and in his last hours would be air-hammering a fence or banging on something.

In the middle of his imaginary play-acting, he stopped, looked up at the ceiling, and said, "Wow, that man is really tall!"

He died the next day. It was the same exact reference Katie made about a tall man in her room.

We continued for a while to pray and sing, praising God for Katie's vitals becoming stable. Then, to our utter dismay, her vitals started to go downhill.

Katie barely lifted her mask and said, "I love you, Dad."

Wes began pleading with God to heal her.

During this time, The Lord spoke to me and said, *If I allow her to live, she will struggle with this the rest of her life.*

I felt panicky. A huge war was going on inside me. My heart was breaking at the thought of letting her go. How could I possibly let her go? Should I continue my fight to keep her here? *Could* I keep her here? Did she even want to stay here?

I couldn't take watching her suffer any longer. Letting go of Katie was the hardest thing I have ever done. I saw a tear roll down her cheek. She knew she was about to leave her family and this earth behind. I wiped her tear away. I wiped my tears away.

No matter how much or hard I prayed, fasted, sang praises, or fought for her, I realized that it wasn't up to me if she lived or died. It just wasn't up to me.

LAST BREATH

Her breathing was shallow, and her heartbeat slowed way down. In a flash, all five of us saw her body go from pink to grey as we watched her spirit leave.

"Her skin feels like sandpaper," Wes said.

I felt the scratchiness of her arm, too. I thought, *Her body is turning back to dust.*

Just like that, she was gone. The song playing at the time was "In His Presence," and that's where Katie was. My husband wouldn't give up and was still pleading for God to heal her.

After a few minutes, I composed myself enough to get the words out, "Honey, let her go. She's with Jesus now, and she won't ever have to suffer again."

He laid his head on her chest and wept. I kissed her frail hand and held it to my wet cheek. I felt disbelief wash over me. Katie's heart was involuntarily beating about every 20 seconds, and she took a few slow breaths, but she was different. I knew she wasn't there.

I stepped outside the room where Consuelo had been waiting all night and told her it was time. Consuelo quietly came in and gave her the high dose of morphine. Katie sucked in her last breath and flat-lined. Consuelo unhooked all the machines.

It was quiet now, except for everyone's hushed weeping. Our fight was over. I felt like I was outside of my own body. I stood there staring at her, frozen, holding my breath. I felt like I had just died, too. It would have been easier if I had. I remember telling myself, *Breathe…just breathe!*

Wes wept as he sat on the bed next to Katie, picked her up, and held her one last time. I don't know why I didn't—maybe because I knew she wouldn't hug me back—I don't know. Oh, how I wished I had hugged her one last time. I regretted that, and, later on, it would affect me in a very negative way.

PARTING WORDS

Consuelo told me that, at first, she didn't want to get close to Katie, because she had become close to a little boy who died, and she just couldn't handle going through that again. But, she went on to say that she was so glad she got to know Katie and would never forget her, because she was such a special child. I told her to never stop taking a chance on pouring her life into these sick kids, because they needed her. I told her how much we appreciated all she did for Katie.

It was around 6:00 a.m., and Elayne and Debbie began to tear down her room where we had lived the past 30 days. There was so much stuff that it filled three cars. The doctor on call that morning was Dr. Bertuch.

She said to me, "Mrs. Herndon, I'm just so sorry. We did everything we could for your daughter."

"I know you did," I said. "and I really appreciate everything you did, but it was it was out of your hands, and it was out of our hands. She belongs to God, and she's with Him now." I wiped the flood of tears from my face. I told the doctor I wanted to clean Katie's body before sending her downstairs.

Wes left to call our family and close friends and tell them the news. Elayne and I began washing her hair and bathing her. Someone asked me once how I could possibly do that, and I think it was because I knew Katie was no longer there. At this point, I was just going through the motions, anyway. Elayne helped me dress her, and someone came and loaded her body onto the gurney, covered her with a sheet, and wheeled her out. It was eerie seeing my daughter looking like she was in a *CSI* episode.

I was so thankful it was too early in the morning for any of the other children on the floor to be awake. I didn't want them to be traumatized by seeing her. I walked out into the hallway where the nurses were waiting for me to come out. We had gotten to know all of them over the past month, and they were all hugging us and giving us their condolences. ♠

CHAPTER 20

FAITH ASSAULTED

Wes and I decided to tell Bethany and Nick in person. Bethany was staying with a friend, so I called the mom and let her know about Katie. I told her we were coming by to pick Bethany up but not to say anything to her. The mom had to wake Bethany up when we got there. She came stumbling out of the house and got into the back seat. I slid in next to her, not saying a word. She knew something was up, since Wes and I were together.

She asked me, "Mom, where's Katie?"

I just looked at her without saying a word. She could see it in my face. She shook her head no and started to cry. I started crying, too, and held her.

"Why didn't you tell me before, so I could be up there with her to say goodbye?" she asked.

"I was trying to protect you," I said.

She started sobbing, "No, Mom."

We got home, and Nick was still asleep. We walked into his room to tell him. Wes sat down next to him. Nick and Katie were very close, and he took it very hard. He never said a word; he just rolled over and wept. He didn't leave his bedroom for 30 hours.

As parents, sometimes we make bad decisions. This would qualify as a bad decision. On one hand, we thought we were protecting Nick and Bethany. On the other hand, Wes and I were entrenched in warfare for our youngest daughter's life. We knew we had to be focused. We were up all night fighting for her, and I don't think either Nick or Bethany were in a place of maturity to do that kind of warfare. However, I know we messed up by not letting them say goodbye to their sister one last time, and I'm sorry for that.

THE HARD QUESTION

It's so hard to put into words how exhausted and drained we were when we got home from the hospital that day. Wes and I both collapsed into bed. I slept a couple of hours and woke up crying and crying, the realization sinking in of what we had lost. I cried so much, I quit developing tears. The crushing weight of grief felt like a thousand tons. I didn't know I was capable of hurting so much.

In the midst of my deepest pain, I heard God ask me again, *Do you trust Me, no matter what?*

It stopped me dead in my tracks. "Really Lord? You expect me to trust You after You took my child from me? Really? I'm not sure I can!" I shouted.

I thought about His question over and over. I thought about our 16-month-long journey and how we saw God do some awesome things in our midst. *Lord, I believed You were able. I believed You were the great physician, our Healer. Even Your word says, "You were bruised for our iniquities, and, by your stripes, we are healed."*

I had believed Katie would be healed, but this wasn't the outcome I was expecting. It caused me to stop and do some very deep soul-searching. I had to ask myself, *Is all this faith stuff just a myth? Does God really love me, and can I ever trust Him again? Will I?* I was simmering in anger and deep grief all at the same time. It felt like my faith had been assaulted. I didn't answer His question and wasn't sure if I could ever trust Him again.

SUNDAY

Elayne got the word out that we weren't taking any visitors until Sunday. Food began arriving and flowers, too. A lot of people began arriving the next day. I really appreciated their condolences, but I was still so exhausted from what we had been through.

Her Memorial service was set for Tuesday. My in-laws had an extra cemetery plot they were giving us, so we buried her in south Texas. Debbie Schultz came over to pick up some of Katie's favorite things to display on a table at the service in a tribute to her. Duncan agreed to do the officiating. People organized a sit-down dinner for the family before the funeral.

Dodie Osteen sat next to me while we ate. I felt honored that she would even come. She asked me, "Valerie, why do you think Katie died?"

I was surprised by her question, but she knew how much we had believed God for a miracle, and, yet, Katie still died. Even she was baffled.

I said, "You know, Dodie, I'm not really sure. I know Katie had enough faith, we did, and so did you. I think she was just so tired of fighting, and once she got a glimpse of heaven, all she wanted was to go home."

It was the best answer I could come up with, but I still believe it to be true after all these years. ♠

CHAPTER 21

HONORING KATIE

W hen Cindy Cruse-Ratcliff got the news about Katie, she offered to sing for the memorial service from her CD that we had listened to over and over. We were so grateful when she sang "In His Presence" and "I Want to See Your Glory." It was beautiful to hear the songs in person that we loved and meant so much to us. Some friends had put together funny video clips of Katie growing up and just being Katie, and it was all such a blessing. There were so many people. Nick and Bethany got up and both talked about their sister. I don't think I could have done it. It was a beautiful ceremony and honored Katie perfectly. God's grace gave us the strength to get through it all.

The next day, we got up to make the five-hour drive to south Texas. When we got there, the first thing we did was go to the funeral home to pick out a casket. Let me just say, I have always had the creeps just going into funeral homes. I prefer closed casket funerals to open casket, but that's just my preference. So, it was a gut-wrenching experience picking out the right coffin for Katie. Parents shouldn't have to pick out coffins for their children.

We picked out a tombstone and had them engrave the picture of the angel she had drawn carrying the little girl in her arms. We also had her scripture, 2 Corinthians 4:15-18, engraved at the top. At the graveside, Wes's longtime friends were there with our family, along with many people from the Rio Grande Valley paying their respects. There were some who drove down from Houston, too. Our family was grateful for the outpouring of support, and, to this day, I don't blow off going to funerals.

I often hear people say, "I just don't like going to funerals." I used to say that, too, but I realized it wasn't about how it affected me, but it was about showing your support for the bereaved family.

Our brother-in-law, Dries, and Wes's sister, Beth, did the graveside. They told a few stories and talked candidly about Katie. I still had a hard time accepting that her body was in that pink metallic casket. It would be a very long time before I accepted Katie's death. After the crowd dwindled, I told Wes I was going to wait in the car. It was a steamy, hot afternoon, so I left the door open. Wes said goodbye to the last few people. He got into the car but had forgotten something, so he slid out of his seat, leaving the driver's side door open. I was staring at the dashboard in a daze when this dragonfly flew into the car on my side. It hovered in front of me, did a loop-the-loop, and flew out Wes's side.

I couldn't believe my eyes. Katie loved dragonflies. She used to draw them a lot. Her nickname in sixth grade was "Draggo," and, every time I see one, I think of her. I knew it was a small token of

God's love for me, that He had not forgotten me, and of His assurance that I would see Katie again very soon. ♣

CHAPTER 22

TRYING TO PICK UP THE PIECES

A week had passed since Katie's death. The phone rang, and it was Melody calling to give her condolences. As soon as she asked me how I was doing, I began to weep. Melody had become my friend in the past 16 months, and I instantly connected her voice to Katie and all we had been through together.

"You know, Valerie, I said I was concerned about all this miracle stuff, but I have to tell you, I did see a miracle," Melody said. "Katie lived 30 more days than she was physically supposed to. There was no way she should have made it out of ICU."

"Yeah, she surprised us all," I said. I finally had to ask Melody the hard question. I was dreading her answer. I took a deep breath and asked, "Melody, do you think Katie would have lived if we had decided to do more chemo?"

She immediately said, "No. That was such a fast-moving cancer that nothing was going to stop it."

I was so relieved to hear her say that, because we played the "what if" game with that one big time. I thought about her last four months and how happy those days were. We probably would not have had that gift if she had been doing treatments again. I also told Melody I could have done without that last meeting describing Katie's death day. She agreed and said that doctor could have softened it a little bit.

I was so glad she called. These days, she works in palliative care helping ease the suffering of children who have cancer. I recently caught up with her after 12 years, and she told me that she has seen a lot of children die in her career. She also said that some of the kids stick out in her mind more than others, and Katie was one of them. She remembered her sweet nature and how she kept her sense of humor even in extremely stressful situations. Melody was—and still is—an awesome human being.

DEAD INSIDE

I didn't enjoy the usual things anymore. I didn't feel anything. What prayers I did toss up to God felt heavy, like they didn't even get past the ceiling. I just didn't care. To me, dying would have been so much easier than living. Even my marriage felt dead.

I shouted at God, *What's the use? This is too much for me! I can't do this!*

He was silent.

Lord, where are You? I would ask. I desperately needed help. I was incapable of doing this alone. God, in His infinite grace, surrounded us with a church and people who were there to help us find our way back to healing. We were even helped by a professional psychologist.

We did what was needed to receive healing in ourselves and our marriage, too.

This was a very long, slow process. It took me 11 years before I could even watch videos of Katie. ◖

CHAPTER 23

JEREMIAH 29:11

I have always loved the scripture in Jeremiah 29:11 where it says: "'For I know the plans I have for you,' says the Lord. 'They are plans for good and not for disaster, to give you a future and a hope.'" What I never identified with until now was in verses 4-6:

The Lord Almighty, the God of Israel, sends this message to all the captives He exiled to Babylon from Jerusalem. Build homes, and plan to stay. Plant gardens, and eat the food you produce. Marry, and have children. Then, find spouses for them, and have many grandchildren. Multiply! Do not dwindle away! (NLT)

God was telling his people who had been held captive in Babylon to keep on living, even though they were prisoners in a foreign country. We felt captive going through our daughter's cancer, and now it felt like we were being held captive in grief's grip. God was telling us to keep on living and not dwindle away. Unaware of what God was doing behind the scenes, we were about to be blown away by His goodness like never before.

THE LAND

About ten days after Katie died, I decided to clean up some of the clutter around the house. We had this big cabinet in the dining room where I used to keep all the kids' drawings and craft supplies. When I opened one of the drawers, I saw a picture Katie had drawn when she was six years old. It was a house with smiling stick figures in the yard. There were some jumbled up letters scribbled across the top. Whenever I couldn't make out what Katie had written, I would ask her what it said and then write it on the back of her art. I flipped it over, and on the back I had translated, "This is your dream castle." I didn't think much about it, except that it seemed odd that her drawing was left behind. I had emptied out those drawers several years ago and stored all the kids' art in the attic.

A few days later, my friend, Debra Parker, called. "Hey, would you like to go with me to look at some orchids?" She asked.

"Sure," I said. "I'm not doing anything else, anyway." It would be good to get out of my quiet, empty house.

"Would you like to see the property we just bought?" she asked. "It's a development outside of town we stumbled

upon." We drove into a beautiful area that I had never seen before with huge pecan trees everywhere.

"Wow, I really like this area. Can you drive around some more? Maybe there's more land for sale."

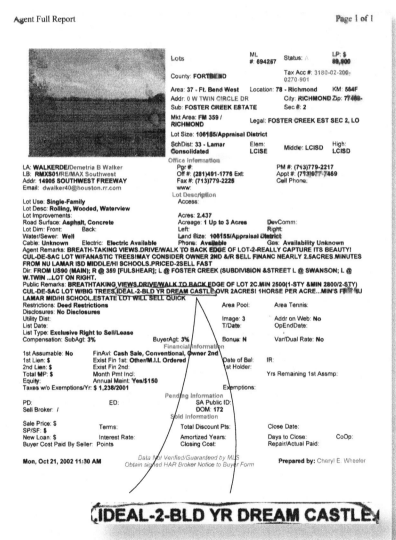

Wes and I had been asking God for 23 years for property out in the country. We used to drive around on weekends looking at land and could never agree on anything. Debra and I came to a cul-de-sac, and there tucked away was this beautiful property for sale. There were huge pecan trees scattered about the 2 ½ acres and pecans on the ground as thick as carpet. It sat on Jones Creek. I jumped out of the car and grabbed a flyer listing all the details of the property. I stuck it in my purse and didn't look at it until I got home by myself.

Later at home, I began reading all the details about the land. I couldn't believe my eyes. There in the realtor's description it read, "Ideal to build your dream castle."

I started crying and called Wes at work. "I found our property," I said. He was skeptical, until I told him about Katie's picture and the flyer. Later that day, we drove out to the property. It was everything we dreamed of and more.

There were huge vines of wild grapes that hung from the pecan trees close to the creek. I wondered what the children of Israel were looking at the first time they laid eyes on their Promised Land. We started imagining where we would build the house and dreaming of all the things we could grow. My husband is slow-moving and logical in his approach to life; he balances me well. Even he couldn't hide his enthusiasm.

All he said was, "I like it." It was the first time we ever agreed on a property in 23 years.

The next day, I was working out at the Y with Cheryl Wheeler, my friend and realtor. During bicep curls, I casually mentioned the property.

She said, "Put an offer on it."

I was hesitant and said, "Today?"

She said, "Yes, after we get done, I'll call their realtor."

The first thing I thought was I needed my husband's approval, and he doesn't rush into anything. To my surprise, when I told him what Cheryl said, he said to go ahead, but to offer less than the asking price. So, Cheryl called their realtor with our offer, but she said there was a contingency offer on the land right now, which meant others were going to buy it if they could sell their house. A few days later, the realtor said they accepted our offer, and the land was going to be ours! They didn't even counter!

THE CLOSING

When it was time to close on the property, we walked into the realtor's office and met the couple who was selling the land. The woman was very friendly, but the man was sullen and refused to make eye contact. He never uttered a word, not even a hello. We sat down at the table across from the man, his arms crossed and his eyes looking down. The rest of us were all making friendly small talk.

Finally, he looked up at us and said flatly, "I hope you know you're getting a beautiful piece of property."

I couldn't hold back my enthusiasm and said, "I know! I can't believe you're selling it!"

My husband about croaked when I said that and wanted me to be quiet since we hadn't signed the dotted line yet. Wes was afraid the man might change his mind.

The man didn't respond, but his realtor spoke up and said, "Well, it's sort of a touchy subject." Then, she went on to explain how her client at one time had five businesses, but with the downturn in the economy, he had to sell them all off. They were expecting their third child, which was a surprise to them, and didn't have time to build a house on the property, because they needed a bigger house right away. He'd held onto the land as long as he could. She went on to say he had turned down so many offers on the land.

"Well, why did you decide to take our offer?" I asked.

He wouldn't look at me or answer, but the realtor spoke up and said, "It was the right time."

I thought about all the events leading up to this day. I thought about how long we had believed God for this dream to come to pass. I thought about Katie saying she was going to buy us a house in the country with a cottage garden. I began sharing with the group, not even knowing where they stood in knowing Jesus.

"We've been asking God for 23 years for a house in the country. Our youngest daughter, Katie, was our third child and was also a surprise baby. We just lost her to cancer a month ago." My voice cracked. "She meant so much more to us than our dream of a house in the country." Then, I asked the realtor, "How often do you use the phrase, 'Build your dream castle here?'"

She said, "I've never used that phrase before."

I told them about finding the dream castle picture after Katie died. By then, the woman selling, the realtor, and I were all crying.

The man softened his shoulders, unclasped his hands, and said, "Well, if I have to sell the property, I'm glad that a Christian couple is getting it."

We never saw them again. I said a prayer for them that God would bless them with something even better than the land they gave up and that He would especially bless them with the special surprise coming their way. Anytime someone visits us, we pull out Katie's drawing and the flyer and tell them the story. God truly amazed us that day. ♦

CHAPTER 24

MOVING ON

After closing on the property, Wes and I would spend countless hours there. We felt such a connection to the land. When Katie's sixteenth birthday rolled around, we decided to plant a bur oak on the front of the property in her honor. While we were digging the hole, a truck pulled up. A man and woman got out of the pickup and introduced themselves as Eddie and Monetta Reyes. They started asking about us and how many kids we had.

That's a question I finally learned how to answer. We say we have three, give their ages, and then say our youngest is in heaven. It sounds better than saying Katie died of cancer. If people want to know more, then we tell them; if not, we just move on. This couple wanted to know more.

Monetta asked where Katie had gone to school. She smiled and said, "My son knew your daughter!" That was pretty amazing, since Katie had attended the new high school only five days. There were almost 1,500 students there. We talked some more, and the subject of where we attended church came up.

When we told her, her eyes got really big, and she said, "You're *that* couple!"

"What couple?" I asked.

"The couple whose daughter was in the hospital who listened to the Cindy Cruse-Ratcliff CD over and over," she said. "I sang on that CD!"

We both started to cry. I thought, *Lord, here is one of the women who used her gift to equip us with your presence and strength, and she is my new neighbor!* Twelve years later, she would be instrumental in helping me publish this book. Lord, You are amazing!

SELLING THE HOUSE KATIE GREW UP IN

The time came to face leaving the house Katie grew up in. We put it on the market, and it sold in ten days. It was not a seller's market, either. But, when God says it's time to move, it's time to move.

Katie was a world-class pack rat. I found so much stuff squirreled away under her bed, in her closet, and in her drawers. She kept everything anyone had ever given her. It was hard throwing some of the stuff away, especially knowing it had meant something to her. But, in order for us to move forward, I had to get the house cleaned up. I kept the valuable items of Katie's, some clothing of hers, toys for my future grandchildren, and sold the rest in a garage sale or gave it away. This was so hard to do, but I just didn't want truckloads of non-essential items taken with us.

I also needed to find a rental house for us to live in while our new home was being built. Rental property was very high at the time. I did find a decent place in our price range, and when Cheryl called about it, it was already leased out. There just wasn't much to choose from that we could afford.

Wes's boss, Bobby Waid, found out what was going on and offered his home that was currently vacant because they had just bought a new house. Wes blew him off, thinking there was no way we could afford to rent his place. I told Wes to ask him anyway, so he did.

Wes asked Bobby, "How much would you rent your place for?"

"For you, Wes, nothing," Bobby said. "You can live there for free. The only stipulation is it'll be on the market, and, if it sells, you'll have to move out."

We talked it over that evening and decided to take a chance on it. It was a beautiful 3,600 square foot home with a pool in a gated neighborhood. Ironically, we moved on our wedding anniversary. When we finished unloading in the blistering heat, we decided to take a break out back by the pool. I sat down in the chaise lounge and closed my eyes.

A few seconds later, I heard, "Hello? Is anyone here?"

I could not believe my ears. We were there all of ten minutes, and the realtor had shown up at the house with a potential buyer. I began asking God if we had made a mistake. We had many such visits throughout the year we were there. Fortunately, it didn't sell until ten days after we moved out. It really was a test of our faith, but I'm not surprised God held off selling it until we moved into our new home. It was a blessing living in that beautiful place until our dream castle was built. We are still very grateful to Bobby and Janet Waid for their generosity towards our family.

The day finally came when we were able to move into our new

home. That morning, I decided at the last second to pull the drawers out of the big cabinet to make it easier for the movers to load it into their truck. When I pulled the drawer out, I noticed a white paper stuck to the inside of the back panel. I peeled it off, turned it over, and saw a picture from a coloring book of a castle that Katie had colored when she was younger. She had written "hello!" across the top of it in crayon.

Katie would have turned sixteen that day, and Wes and I felt like it was her way of saying, "Celebrate my birthday in your new dream castle!"

God's grace was poured out on us in an unforgettable way that day.

SOME NORMALCY

Bethany's high school team advanced in the playoffs and was competing for the state title about a month after Katie died. What was once so important to us seemed trivial these days. Watching Bethany play, however, did help us feel a little normal for a while. When it came time for the state match, right before they stepped onto the court to play, Bethany told the team what Katie said about winning state for her. The team got very emotional and very motivated to win.

It was a tight match, and Bethany was up to serve. The crowd was deafening. People were all on their feet. We needed all five points to win the title. She served, and won all five points, the last two being aces. One of her teammates said it spelled K-A-T-I-E!

The crowd went wild. The whole team attacked Bethany, and everyone in the stands was crying. Coach Schelfhout said that game would have an eternal impact on her and the team, and that they would remember that day the rest of their lives. And we all still do!

A reporter from San Antonio heard about Katie and interviewed Bethany right after the game. The story also ran in the *Houston Chronicle*. Her team was on a local TV station, and Bethany told the story of winning it for Katie. Her junior year, she was named to the all-state tournament team, MVP of her high school team, and also MVP of the district. She also realized her dream of playing for a Division I college. She received a scholarship that paid for all four years.

But, even with all the exciting things happening around us, it just didn't seem to be that important anymore. It did help take our minds off of our pain for the moment, and we sensed God's love and goodness. ♦

CHAPTER 25

My Own Battle

My days were empty. My purpose of taking care of Katie was snatched away. I felt hopeless and dead. I was home alone during the day, and the house was eerily quiet.

On one hand, I was thankful when I would think about building our new home in the country with a cottage garden. On the other hand, it didn't bring me much comfort. Nothing did, actually. I neglected my own health while tending to Katie and was still neglecting it even though she was gone. I just stopped caring.

However, my body would no longer allow me to ignore it, because I was having my menstrual flow, and it wouldn't stop. I had been bleeding for three weeks straight, so I made an appointment with my gynecologist. She found lumps in my abdomen and both breasts.

"Have you been through any trauma recently?" She asked.

I started crying and said, "Yes, my daughter just died of cancer a couple of months ago."

"Your body is reacting to the trauma of losing your daughter," she said. "I want you to have a mammogram and an ultrasound on your uterus done right away. I'm also referring you to a surgeon for a biopsy on your breasts."

There's that word again! Biopsy. I felt uneasy just hearing that word. I knew what it could mean, but, this time, I faced it head on. I wasn't afraid of death any more. I just didn't want to suffer like Katie did.

Something rose up in me that day: a kind of anger, a righteous indignation. I was angry that Katie was gone. It came from deep down, and I screamed at the enemy like I did when Katie was sick.

I yelled, "Devil, I don't care if I live or die! I win either way, and you lose. If I live, I stay here and serve Jesus, and, if I die, I go to heaven and spend eternity with Him and Katie! You lose! Did you hear me, stupid devil? You lose! So, take your best shot!" I shouted it as loud as I could. Even my toenails were mad. I meant every word, because it was the truth. I felt such hatred and anger towards that evil chump. I told God when it came time for Him to finally put the devil in the slimy pit where he belonged, I wanted a crack at him. I had visions of kicking him in the face and stomping on his puny little head.

After I settled down, I resigned that as long as God was leaving me here on this earth, I would start paying attention to my own health and taking better care of myself. Besides, I still had a husband who needed me and two very beautiful children who I loved dearly.

The day came for my biopsy, and my friend, Debra Parker, went with me. I went in to see the surgeon and sat down in the chair.

She started gathering information on me and then looked at me and said, "Mrs. Herndon, have you been through any trauma lately?"

Same question the gynecologist asked me. I told her about Katie.

"No wonder you're having problems," she said. "I don't think it's necessary to do a biopsy just yet. Let's try to get your bleeding under control and stress levels down. Go do something fun, and I'll follow up with you in a few weeks."

The doctor's instincts were right. I felt an ache in my chest, and it wasn't physical. It was an ache that came from not getting any more hugs from Katie. My nurturing, life-giving parts were ravaged when she died, and I truly believe part of the reason was a result of not hugging her one last time. How I regretted not doing that, and it affected me in a very deep way.

My friend Debra was anxiously waiting for me to come out. When we walked out into the hallway, she grabbed my arm and asked with urgency, "What'd the doctor say?"

I couldn't help myself, but I felt like being mischievous. I stopped, looked her square in the face, and said, "The doctor wants to cut my boob off."

She gasped and said, "Oh, Valerie! No!"

I held my stare for about five seconds and couldn't keep a straight face any longer. I started to laugh.

She looked at me in disbelief and said, "Valerie! Are you kidding me? I can't believe you just did that"

I laughed harder. She didn't think it was very funny, which made me laugh even more. Debra was the butt of my humor that day, but I felt a spark of life again, even if it was for a brief moment.

About a week later, the bleeding stopped. The lumps started shrinking in my breasts and uterus a couple of months later. I began eating better, exercising, and depending on the Lord whenever my thoughts would turn negative. I was extra careful about what

I watched on TV or listened to on the radio. I still to this day have a hard time watching a drama series where people are dying. I prefer to watch comedies, as long as they're not crude or vulgar. I enjoy hanging out with funny people, because it has helped me in the healing process. God has surrounded me with friends and family who have great senses of humor. The Bible says that laughter is like a medicine, and I believe that. I also believe it was important that I do my part and then allow God to do His part.

PULLED OUT OF THE PIT

I found myself asking God to help me with the deep, emotional pain I was still feeling after four months. We were at church in the middle of praise and worship, and God gave me a vision. I saw Him pulling me out of a very dark pit by the hand and placing me in his glorious light. I turned a corner that day, and it started my road to healing.

COMFORTED

I have to confess something that some will relate to and others will think is strange, but it helped me in my grief. My husband didn't have these experiences.

After Katie died, I would have these conversations with her—not out loud, but in my head. I guess I was so used to talking to her on a daily basis that it just seemed to come naturally. I could hear her responding to me, and it was quite comforting. Some may even think it was the enemy pretending to be Katie, but I don't believe he's smart enough to hear what I'm thinking. I've had people tell me it might have been the Holy Spirit talking to me, but I don't think God's Holy Spirit would pretend to be my daughter, either. To be honest, I don't really know for sure if it was Katie or not.

One thing I do believe is that God was allowing those conversations for a season, because He knew it would be a comfort to me. However, after a few months of this, I felt the conviction of the Holy Spirit telling me that I spent more time talking to Katie than to Him, which was true. He was showing me that I was seeking her more than Him, and that I was putting her before Him. It was during this time that I didn't sense His presence as much, either. For a while, I had stopped seeking Him as much as Katie. I longed to hear His voice again and missed having His presence near me. So, I started having my conversations with God more and more and conversations with Katie less and less. I am sharing this to tell others to be careful if you are conversing with your deceased loved one. It is very easy to make them into an idol.

One day, several months after we started building our new home, I was sitting out on the hill overlooking Jones Creek behind us. I felt Katie lay her head on my shoulder like she used to do. Another time, it was early spring; the soft breeze was blowing, birds were singing, and everything was beginning to turn green. This peaceful place was our healing therapy.

I took in a deep breath and told Katie, "You should see this place."

I heard her say, *No, Mom, you should see this place!*

I laughed and thought she was right. Nothing can compare to heaven.

I don't have those experiences with Katie or any of the conversations anymore. My conversations are with the Lord these days, and He is always near me. I do have dreams about Katie. They are happy dreams, and, when I wake up and remember them, it's as if we have spent actual time together. I know they are gifts from the Lord, and I'm very thankful for them. ♦

CHAPTER 26

LAUGHING AGAIN

We still miss her after 12 years of life without her. I know a sweet elderly lady whose son has been gone over 50 years, and she said it's something you never fully get over. But, we had to come to grips with our loss, even if all of our questions never got answered. We had to pick up the pieces that were left and keep going. We had to learn a new normal.

I remember how odd it felt to belly laugh the first time after Katie's death, how I felt guilty for having a moment of happiness again. I had to realize that the Lord wanted me to live joyfully again and that He enjoyed my laughter. I had to think of God as a parent in this part of the healing process.

For example, the summer before Katie died, she was downstairs with her brother and sister looking at something on the computer. They all just burst out laughing about something silly they had just seen. Wes and I were upstairs watching TV. He turned down the volume, and we just sat there savoring that moment and soaking in their laughter. It had been a very long time since we had heard the kids all enjoying themselves so much. It is still a sweet memory for us both. It helped me realize how much the Father enjoys His children laughing and having fun, too.

RESTORED

When a couple loses a child, there may be blame towards their spouse, or they may feel let down and disappointed by them. Or, they may be eaten up with guilt from their child dying. If the marriage wasn't strong before the traumatic events, it can have catastrophic effects afterwards. I felt all those things. Wes and I needed to forgive each other. I needed to forgive Wes for burying himself in work or disconnecting from me emotionally. It was his way of coping. He needed to forgive me of my unrealistic expectations. I had expected him to help me in the healing process even more than he was. Wes could only do so much. He needed healing, too. Even though he is the only human who can understand my grief fully, he is limited by his humanness. What I needed was a supernatural touch from God to heal me like only He could. It was a process that I am still walking out every day. It's just not as intense as it used to be. Wes and I were—and still are—a comfort to each other, but only God could heal us.

Losing Katie brought Wes and I closer. It was an answer to a prayer I always had hidden in my heart that God would make our marriage stronger and bring us closer together. But, this wasn't exactly what I had pictured in my mind. He has taken what is a very huge loss in our lives and made something beautiful out of it. I'm so thankful we have each other.

Losing Katie also brought us closer as a family, too. It brought healing in Nick and Bethany's relationship, as well. But, the biggest benefit of all was our family becoming closer to the Lord in the process. Satan tried to use the loss of our youngest child to wreck our faith in God, but it did just the opposite for us. It made us realize how much we depended on Him and needed Him on a daily—sometimes moment-by-moment—basis.

My hope and prayer is that Wes and I can grow really old together. We're best friends now. I prefer to hang out with him more than anyone. These days, we teach a marriage class in our Sunday school at church. We have been amazed at how much God has used our experiences to help others who are hurting. We count it a privilege and have met some of the best people in the world there. Our relationship with each other and with our children is an example to many of God's grace being poured out on our family.

KEEPING IT ALL IN PERSPECTIVE

One thing among many things Katie's death has taught us is how to keep everything in perspective. Her death is what we measure every trial by. Believe me when I say, it keeps us from being too petty about unimportant things. Life really is too short to sweat the small stuff, and everything compared to her death is the small stuff.

One of the things people say to me is, "How do you ever get over losing your child?"

My response is, "You don't." There isn't a day that goes by that she doesn't cross our minds in some way. That hole will always be there, because she was such a huge part of our lives. But, the hope that we have of seeing her again gives us comfort.

Another thing people say to me is, "I don't think I could handle losing my child."

I used to say the same thing. It's because people who have never lost a child don't need God's grace in that area. The only way we have made it is by God's abundant grace.

Jesus said, "My grace is sufficient for you" (2 Corinthians 12:9a).

He is faithful to give us the strength we need for whatever it is we're going through at the moment. It's a free gift, and He loves giving it to those who ask for it. ⬥

CHAPTER 27

Is Having More Faith the Answer?

I sometimes get irritated with preachers who say that all you need to receive healing from God is to have more faith. I also used to think that, to an extent. I have made the mistake of saying that to a mom whose child was dying, not realizing her personal situation and what God was trying to accomplish in her.

Now, the Bible says that without faith, it is impossible to please God. So, I know I need to have faith in order to please God. The Bible also says that all I need is faith the size of a mustard seed. Who am I that I can judge the amount of someone else's faith? Besides, that doesn't mean God is our big Santa Claus. He's so much more than that. God is more interested in my relationship with Him than in giving me everything I desire.

In 1 John 3:2, it says, "Now beloved, I wish above all things that you prosper and be in health, *even as your soul prospers.*" (Emphasis mine.)

We have a tendency to focus on the first part of that scripture and ignore the second half of it. God is interested in my soul prospering more than anything.

Now, there are many scriptures on healing. I believe in God's healing power, and I know without a doubt that He answers our prayers for healing. I believe it is His will for us to be healed. I have asked God for healing many times, and He answered each prayer. But, what overrides God healing someone on this earth is His sovereign will in his or her life. His or her assignment may be done. He always has a higher plan, though we may not always understand it. There isn't anything we go through without His approval, and He is ultimately in control of our lives.

Do I have all the answers to why Katie died? No, I don't, and I won't pretend that I do. I could run myself crazy trying to figure it all out. I may never fully know the reason this side of heaven, and that's okay. All I do know is, God was and is and always will be with me, and one day I will spend all eternity with Him (and Katie, too).

MY OWN GUILT

I had another issue to work through: I wondered if maybe I had some unconfessed sin in my life, and that was the reason for Katie's death. But, I confessed every sin I could ever remember early on when Katie was diagnosed. The enemy would hit me with guilt and condemnation because of past sin in my life. I had to realize that as long as I am alive, I have the opportunity to sin every day, but God's grace covers me.

None of us are without spot or blemish. None of us deserve anything good in and of ourselves. It's only because of His goodness that we are blessed. It's because of His goodness that He doesn't give us what we really deserve. It's because of His grace and mercy that God doesn't wipe us all out. I seriously don't know how God puts up with humanity.

PROCESSING OUR GRIEF

People process grief in their own ways and in their own time. I always tell people there is no set time to heal from losing a loved one. In our grieving process, the key is to keep moving forward and making progress. There are five stages in grief: disbelief, anger, bargaining (the "what if" stage), depression, and acceptance. Also, don't allow someone else to tell you what amount of time it may take you to heal. I had someone tell me it takes a year. It took me a lot longer than that. I know my husband processed his grief a little differently, too.

If you are stuck and feel you need grief counseling, then why not get it? Sometimes, we need professional help. Or, find someone who has gone through it who can help you through the process. Keeping it inside can be very destructive. Talking does help. The key is to keep moving through each stage until you get to acceptance. It's not unusual to slide back into a previous stage, either. The key is to not stay there. I can't stress that enough.

FIRST ANNIVERSARIES

One thing I was caught off guard about was going through all the "firsts" without Katie. I wish someone would have warned me about what was ahead in this part of the grieving process, so I am sharing this with you.

It was extremely difficult going through the first anniversary of her death, the first Thanksgiving without her, or what would have been her sixteenth birthday. I felt a void when school was out the following spring, and I didn't register her for summer camp. No more orthodontist appointments or getting her favorite foods at the store or taking her to youth group.

That first Christmas after she died, well-meaning friends pooled their finances together for our family to spend Christmas in Colorado. It was good to get away, and we really appreciated their thoughtfulness. However, I was caught off guard by my pain the second Christmas without Katie. I realized it was because I hadn't walked through it yet. I knew I had to walk through every one of our "first" anniversaries if I wanted to be healed of my grief.

I couldn't ignore my emotions, because that would only prolong my grief. That meant whenever I would have a meltdown, I would allow myself to cry or get angry. I knew that for me to get through all the pain, I had to finally accept the fact she wasn't coming back. My dreams for her were lost, and thoughts of her not graduating high school, getting married, and having children would depress me.

I then learned to lean on the Lord for help to get me through, and He would carry me until I felt the wave of grief pass. I also realized that even though she was missing out on major milestones on earth, she could care less about them now. She was experiencing so much more than I could ever imagine or think!

TRIGGERS

Anyone who has gone through a huge loss knows immediately what I mean when I say the word *triggers*. It's anything that stirs a deep emotion in you from pain in your past. For me, it was a can of

SpaghettiOs. I was in the grocery store two months after Katie died. When I walked down the aisle and saw the SpaghettiOs, I was overwhelmed with emotion.

I know people walking by thought, "Yeah, that stuff tastes pretty bad, but there's no reason to cry over it!"

It triggered me, because it was the only thing Katie would eat at times during chemo. It was the only time I ever bought the stuff in my entire life. I had associated SpaghettiOs with her.

TRIALS IN THIS LIFE

When I was younger, I avoided reading the book of Job in the Bible. It was so hard for me to wrap my head around a God who would allow so many bad things to happen to a godly man. I didn't have an understanding of what God wanted to accomplish in Job.

After Katie died, I saw things differently and could relate to Job on a much deeper level. For the first time, I began to understand why God allowed the trials in his life. I began understanding why God allows the trials in our lives, too. There is a purpose in them.

Because of the trials we have been through, He has used Wes and me on a much bigger platform than we ever imagined for our own lives. He has used us to strengthen and comfort those He puts in our path. It would be a lot harder to do that if we had never gone through what we did. Now, when we meet someone who has also lost a child, there is an immediate connection without anyone having to say a word. We just know and understand what it's like living without your child. We can identify with someone else's pain.

I think humans have a tendency to overlook all the scriptures on suffering, maybe because they make us uncomfortable. We see life on such a small scale, but God sees the bigger picture. He knows the future, and He has a special plan for each one of our lives. When we go through trials, we have to trust God no matter what. He is worthy of our trust and can bring good out of any bad situation. He did it for the Herndon family and will do it for you, too, no matter what you may be going through.

Sometimes, we think it's unfair to go through hard times, but the early Christians went through hard times. Some were persecuted, jailed, sawed in half, tortured, or even martyred for their faith. Peter was crucified like Jesus, only upside down by his own request. Paul suffered and was eventually beheaded. Are we better than the disciples, the Apostle Paul, or the early Christians? Not hardly. Are we above the trials of life? I used to think so, but not anymore.

When Katie first got diagnosed, I asked God, *Why Katie?*

I heard Him say, *Why not Katie?*

I didn't have an answer. He followed that with 1 Peter 4:12-13:

Beloved, do not think it strange concerning the fiery trial which is to try you, as though some strange thing happened to you; but rejoice to the extent that you partake of Christ's sufferings, that when His glory is revealed, you may also be glad with exceeding joy. (NKJV)

CHAPTER 28

TRUSTING GOD

After many months, I was finally able to answer the Lord's question, Do you trust Me, no matter what?

I said to him, *Yes, Lord, I trust You no matter what, even if I don't understand You. Even when I feel disappointed in You and feel like You didn't come through for me. I know deep down Your ways are higher than mine. I know that Katie was Your creation, not my possession, and that she belonged to You first. She was a gift from You for fifteen years.*

I realized He loved her even more than I did. The Lord did answer our prayers for Katie's healing, just not the way I envisioned. It's so much easier to trust Him when everything is going my way. I believe it takes a much deeper faith to trust in Him when I don't get the outcome I am expecting. I realized that even losing Katie didn't change who God was.

OUR DAYS ARE NUMBERED

I believe God sees death differently than we do.

Paul said, "To live is Christ, but to die is gain."

For those of us who believe in Jesus, we gain heaven when we die. The Bible also refers to this life as a vapor. Life is fleeting.

Katie lived 5,606 days. God knew the number of her days. He knows the number of my days and the number of your days, and each one is a gift. As good as life can be here, it's still no comparison to Heaven. Keeping my eyes towards heaven gives me hope. Thank goodness this is not all there is.

MORE IMPACT

I do know without a doubt that although Katie impacted so many people the last year she was alive, she impacted even more people in her death. When people hear our story, it's not something they can easily brush off or disregard. It affects them. It causes them to stop and think. It gives me a platform to share what God has done for our family with others who are struggling. For that, I'm thankful.

People were so amazed at her strength. Anyone who knew Katie growing up would describe her in words like *sweet* or *kind* or *happy*, not *warrior* or *brave* or *strong*. But, that was the real Katie, and it wasn't obvious until she faced death.

I told her in those last 30 days how I thought she was so brave. Her response was, "I don't feel very brave."

Even so, she faced death—fear and all—and fought a very good fight. She taught us many things, especially in the end. She showed us how to keep our senses of humor and what really matters in this life. She taught us what real faith looks like. She taught us how to look beyond this physical life to see what our eyes couldn't.

Most of all, we have that hope of seeing our daughter in the near future, and I am at peace knowing that no evil will ever touch her again. In the meantime, we are living in an outpouring of God's abundant grace. ♦

EPILOGUE I

WES (DAD)

A special memory I have of Katie happened two months before she died. I decided to take the boat out to go fishing and took Nick and Katie with me. It was time away from the hospital. It felt normal. I appreciated that time so much because she wasn't usually the adventurous type but she still wanted to go. Her and Nick would laugh every time I hit a big wave and we would go airborne. She didn't do any fishing that day, but took her pad and drew the picture above while on the boat.

But, my very favorite memory is the last words Katie ever spoke. Right before she died she said, "I love you, Dad." How I cherish those words.

Even though I spent most of my time at volleyball games with Bethany, my heart was always torn between her games and the hospital. One good thing that happened during that time was my relationship with Bethany was healed. We spent a lot of time together and for that I'm thankful.

I remember after Katie's knee replacement surgery, I carried her upstairs because she was unable to walk on her own. Katie was so concerned with me having to carry her upstairs and was afraid I would hurt my back. But, I was so happy to be able to do it because I felt needed, like I was finally able to help in some way. As a dad I'm supposed to be able to fix everything. Make it better. I couldn't fix this. I wasn't able to make it better. It was outside of my control, something I wrestled with constantly.

I never believed my daughter would die. The thought never crossed my mind. I don't know if you would call that faith or just outright denial. Had I thought she would die, I would have been more deliberate with the amount of time I spent with her.

I have regrets; the biggest is while the kids were growing up. I was always looking for the next season to hurry up and get here instead of savoring each moment I had with them. I was so busy earning a living that I forgot to live.

Now, I am blessed with a beautiful grandson who I adore and have two more on the way. I appreciate every moment I spend with him and can't wait for the rest of them to arrive. They are such a blessing.

I'm very proud of my wife for being so available to devote the time to Katie that she did. I'm proud of my wife for writing this book because I know how much pain she had to relive in order to get it written. It took a lot of work and truly was a labor of love. It's not something I could have done. 🔥

EPILOGUE II

BETHANY

When I was 12 months old, a little girl name Katie Leigh entered this world and stole all of my parents' love and attention. Believing that the world had previously revolved around me, you can understand my confusion.

I persevered, and Katie became my constant companion and partner in crime. I didn't realize it then, but she was my biggest fan. Our early teen years were hard on us, and we drifted apart. My actions towards her during that time would be a huge source of guilt and shame that the Lord would have to deal with later.

When I was told that Katie was diagnosed with cancer, my coping mechanism was to refuse to accept it. It never occurred to me that she could actually die. People survive cancer every day. My parents shielded me from a lot of it, and my life continued on like normal. I am extremely grateful for their sacrifice to both fight for my sister's life and allow me to function as a normal 16-year-old.

There were moments when the veil was lifted, and I got small glimpses into the despair and fight around me. Katie and I shared a bathroom, and I once went in to take a shower after her. She had just started chemo. I found a very large pile of her hair tucked under the bathroom rug. It seemed like it was enough for an entire wig. I knew she was ashamed of it and didn't want to talk about it, so I cleaned it all up and hid it in the bottom of the trash for her.

I pushed the significance of this away and pretended it didn't happen. I tried to make it all a joke. It was my only way of knowing how to cope. Making her laugh again made me feel like she wasn't sick. I was desperate to have my partner back, but I was too immature emotionally to correctly address the severity of the situation.

When she was given 24 hours to live, my life fell apart, and I literally crumbled to the floor. My protective barriers and normalcy were stripped. My sister was nearly dead. That night the greatest, most life-changing shift happened to me.

I looked into the ICU room and witnessed my parents, the Dodds, and Slaters praying over Katie. In that moment, alone outside her room, the Lord broke down even more barriers in my heart. I watched men and women of great faith cling to a sovereign and faithful God, one who graciously met them there in that room of hopelessness and gave them the gift of His presence. I watched my sister be a pillar of faith.

The Lord met me there as well, and a new revelation came, one that quietly asked my heart if that is what my faith looked like. A resounding and crushing "no" filled my head. My "faith" was far from theirs. My faith was in volleyball and the desire to be popular, pretty, and independent (read: wild). When did my little sister begin to reflect Jesus so greatly? When did she begin to have faith greater than anything I had ever imagined?

Her incredibly painful and sanctifying journey of walking with Jesus was ending, but mine was beginning that night. I knew so much about the Lord but had let it affect me very little. I just wanted to make sure I wouldn't go to hell or be left behind after the rapture. I didn't know where to start, so I told Jesus that night that I wanted to look more like Katie, that my life was His, and confessed that I had done a really bad job with it so far. I hated what I thought was important. My sister was fighting for her life and praising Jesus, and I wanted more clothes.

I started with obedience—what I knew was right, but hadn't given much thought to—and asked Jesus to meet me there. He was faithful, and in what little steps I took toward Him, He ran like wildfire towards me.

When Katie passed 30 days later, my life crumbled again. I trusted Jesus but still struggled how to address the deep pain in my heart. I refused to let others see me cry, because I thought it would add to their pain. I remember coming home from school and catching a glimpse of my mom in Katie's bed crying.

I just remember thinking, *I have to be strong for her; I can't make it worse.* So, I hid it all for as long as I could. I cried myself to sleep every night for three months, and then everything held in came flooding out uncontrollably. But, with those tears came words, the ones that had been bottled up about my crushing sadness, about the stabbing guilt I felt, and all that I had witnessed but pushed back. That was the first night I didn't cry myself to sleep but instead began to experience healing.

It was—and is—a very long process. My guilt haunted me for a long time and is still something I have to give over to the Lord. Along with stuffing my sadness came stuffing all emotions. I never told Katie I loved her or hugged her in the last 30 days of her life. I remember standing over her and trying to will myself to kiss her forehead and tell her what she meant to me. Instead, I casually told her I would see her tomorrow. I would end up never seeing her again.

This crushing regret and anger towards myself was suffocating. I convinced myself that if I had expressed my feelings during that time, I could have absolved all of the wrong I had done in the past, all the ways I failed her, mistreated her, and took her for granted. I couldn't forgive myself, and I couldn't accept the Lord's forgiveness, either. I didn't deserve it, and I wanted to punish myself.

Two years later, the Lord gave me a very precious gift. One night, I had a very vivid dream. I was walking through Texas Children's, and Katie was walking towards me. She was wearing all white and walking normally. She had a huge smile on her face. I sprinted towards her and wrapped my arms around her. I kissed her face and told her over and over again how much I loved her. As I hugged her harder, I could *feel* her. I could *smell* her. All at once, I woke up. I still felt warmth on my skin and her smell, just for a moment. The Lord allowed me to say goodbye to her. It is still one of the sweetest gifts He has ever given me. He loves so deeply and intimately.

Every day, I miss my partner in all things. Not having my only sister and deepest friendship has left an aching in my soul. She gave me the greatest gift any human can give another, and that is the gift of introducing me to a personal relationship with Jesus Christ.

One day, we will worship Him together again. 🍂

EPILOGUE III

NICK

Early on in Katie's chemotherapy treatment, when I had just graduated from college and moved back home, I would get frustrated with her—her constant nausea, lethargy, and generally poor attitude. I didn't fully understand the serious nature of Katie's illness and was immature and impatient when interacting with her. I don't recall many outbursts or outward manifestations of my frustration, but it was always close to the surface.

One day while running an errand at work, I grabbed lunch at a fast food drive-through. The hamburger I got was room temperature, but because it was 3:00 in the afternoon and I hadn't eaten all day, I wolfed it down without a second thought. Later that afternoon when I got home, it hit me: the searing abdominal pain, the sweating, the cramps, and, worst of all, the vomiting. I had severe food poisoning.

My mom, dad, and Katie were at the hospital for Katie's treatment, Bethany was away at a friend's house, and I was home by myself, confined to a couch. Every time I tried to sit up or even roll to my side, fresh waves of nausea would wash over me, and I would have to run to the bathroom to vomit. Eventually, I gave up trying to go to the bathroom each time I got sick and kept a trash can by the couch.

This continued for the remainder of the evening and all night, well into the next morning. When I was finally able to hold down water and a little food (crackers, mostly), I began thinking about how poor my attitude had been toward my sister who was living in constant pain and nausea. I could barely handle it for 24 hours; it was her life. In corporate speak, this would be referred to as a "learning opportunity." From that day forward, my attitude changed, and I was able to fully appreciate our time together.

Katie's life prior to cancer was normal, and our sibling relationship was as normal as could be. I was the protective older brother and cared for my baby sister—or, at least, I thought I did. It wasn't until the food poisoning episode that I began to understand the grace and courage she had while walking through this terrible time.

When Katie was sick for the last time and spent her final month at the hospital, I learned what real grace meant. There was a constant influx of doctors, nurses, friends, family, church leaders, well-wishers, curious onlookers, and other assorted folk who visited for a variety of reasons, most of them well-meaning. It was exhausting for my parents, though they rarely complained, and exhausting for Katie, who never complained.

Everyone got to see firsthand Katie's grace and courage. If polled, everyone who visited her room would have almost certainly said that they felt "peaceful" upon leaving. Many, many people who came to visit left and remarked about how peaceful it was in Katie's hospital room. I saw it; my friends who visited saw it. It was Philippians 4:7 come to life ("And the peace of God, which surpasses all understanding, will guard your hearts and your minds in Christ Jesus").

Katie's life with cancer impacted me, but her death profoundly changed my life.

Within the first few days after Katie was gone, I realized that my relationship with Bethany was broken. I'd spent so much time with Katie over the past year that I hardly interacted with Bethany at all. I went to Bethany and told her that I loved her and never thought of her as second to Katie. I apologized for not being a more supportive brother. Our relationship now is in a great place. I am blessed to call Bethany my sister.

After Katie's death, my parents started hugging Bethany and me a lot more. It was a small thing, but now whenever we see each other, we always greet with hugs. I recently admitted to my mom that was something I missed growing up, as neither she nor my dad showed much affection, especially as I got older.

One of the biggest blessings that came out of Katie's death was meeting my wife, Kelly. She had recently lost her mom to cancer and understood the devastating effects of the disease. Both of us agree that it's doubtful that our relationship would have ever progressed beyond a superficial friendship had we not had the shared experience. When talking about our loved ones, we understood each other.

The most significant change to my life happened when my parents delivered the terrible news on the day of Katie's death. I spent that day grieving privately in my room, and, while I was grieving, the Lord spoke to me—not audibly, but He spoke a question into my soul: *Who will you follow? Yourself or Me?*

I grew up in the church and considered myself a Christian who was sincere in his beliefs, but I had never been tested like this. I told Him, *Lord, I've followed You this far; where else would I go?*

Almost immediately, it was as if a fog was lifted and my perspective on death was changed forever. No longer do I see death as the end, but merely as a step toward something greater. Sometimes I am still afraid, and sometimes I doubt, but I now hold a truth deep down in my soul: the truth of Christ and the resurrection. 1 Corinthians 15 says it all:

> *For if the dead are not raised, then Christ has not been raised either. And if Christ has not been raised, your faith is futile; you are still in your sins...But Christ has indeed been raised from the dead, the first fruits of those who have fallen asleep...'Where, O death, is your victory? Where, O death, is your sting?' The sting of death is sin, and the power of sin is the law. But thanks be to God! He gives us the victory through our Lord Jesus Christ.* (NIV)

What I've shared here is a small fragment of the way God has worked in my and my family's lives since Katie died and a tiny glimpse of the blessings He has poured out on us. I miss Katie, but I know that God is sovereign and that His will is perfect, even though people are not. I also know that because of her faith in Jesus, Katie is with Jesus in glory, and I no longer grieve but rejoice that she is beyond the reach of sickness and death.

Shortly after Katie died, I attended a talk by author and pastor Voddie Baucham at a local church. I don't recall most of what he said, but one quote from his sermon has resonated with me ever since: "God is glorified when sick saints are healed," he said, "and God is glorified when sick saints die well."

Amen. 🐚

First Flight

All artwork done by Katie Herndon, mostly during chemo treatments. First Flight was drawn two weeks before she died.